THE PROPHETIC MATRIX
(IN CHRIST)

BY

CATHERINE BROWN

Published by Transparent Publishing

©Transparent Publishing
Published February 2024

ISBN: 9798879109139

Original copyright holder - Catherine Brown

The moral rights of the Author have been asserted.

All rights reserved. No part of this publication may be reproduced, stored in a retrieval system, or transmitted in any form, or by any means, electronic, mechanical, photocopying, recording, or otherwise, without the prior permission of Transparent Publishing or the original copyright holder.

Unless otherwise indicated, Biblical quotations are from the Authorised King James Version of the Bible.
Public Domain.

DEDICATION

To Christ, my all in all, the Giver of all Gifts, the most important of these being new life through Your sacrificial death, resurrection, and ascension.

Contents

- DEDICATION 3
- INTRODUCTION 5
- PART 1 – CHRIST OUR PROPHETIC FOUNDATION 10
- CHAPTER 1 – MOSES AND THE PROPHET TO COME 11
- CHAPTER 2 – PROPHECY FULFILLED IN CHRIST 23
- CHAPTER 3 - ARE THERE STILL PROPHETS AND PROPHECIES TODAY? 28
- CHAPTER 4 – THE MINISTRY OF CHRIST AND THE PROPHETIC 32
- CHAPTER 5 – NOW GOD HAS SPOKEN THROUGH HIS SON 50
- CHAPTER 6 – DISCERNMENT, PERCEIVING, AND KNOWING 57
- PART 2 – THE MATRIX OF THE PROPHETIC IN THE ACTS OF THE APOSTLES 73
- CHAPTER 7 – PROPHECY IN ACTS OF THE APOSTLES 74
- CHAPTER 8 - DREAMS AND VISIONS IN THE NIGHT 90
- CHAPTER 9 – WHAT IS A TRANCE? 106
- CHAPTER 10 - NEW TESTAMENT ENCOUNTERS WITH CHRIST AND WITH ANGELS 117
- CHAPTER 11 – OPEN HEAVEN 131
- CHAPTER 12 - PROPHETIC PREACHING, TEACHING & EVANGELISM 146
- PART 3 – KINGDOM GOVERNANCE 151
- CHAPTER 13 - APOSTOLIC AND PROPHETIC PRESBYTERY 152
- CHAPTER 14 - THE ANTIOCH QUESTION 156
- CHAPTER 15 - BUILDING TOGETHER 168
- CONCLUSION 173
- APPENDICES 179
- ABOUT THE AUTHOR 188
- OTHER BOOKS BY THE AUTHOR 190

INTRODUCTION

Isn't it wonderful to be part of the supernatural realm here on Earth – by being a born again believer and a new creation through Christ in the Kingdom of God!

Let me state my position clearly from the outset: I am not cessationist when it comes to the gift of prophecy, or other spiritual gifts. I do believe that all the gifts of the Holy Spirit are still operational in, and through, the New Testament church and that we can still prophesy today. In fact, I believe we can *all* prophesy according to Apostle Peter's words on the day of Pentecost,

> *17 And it shall come to pass in the last days, saith God, I will pour out of my Spirit upon all flesh: and your sons and your daughters shall prophesy, and your young men shall see visions, and your old men shall dream dreams: 18 And on my servants and on my handmaidens I will pour out in those days of my Spirit; and they shall prophesy: Acts 2:17-18 KJV*

Of course we understand Apostle Peter was quoting the prophecy of Joel, from the Old Testament. Nonetheless, the Scriptures are quite clear that: -

1. In the last days, the Holy Spirit will be poured out on all flesh,
2. Sons and daughters will prophesy,
3. Young men will see visions,
4. Old men will dream dreams,

5. On all the servants of God – both male and female - God will pour out His Spirit,
6. As a result of the outpouring, **they shall all prophesy**.

Simple! Are you sure?

Many times Evangelicals get frustrated with Pentecostal and Charismatic expressions of the church when it comes to spiritual gifts. One of the main reasons for this (though not exclusively), is because the gift is often wrongly given pre-eminence and importance above, and before, the Person of Christ. I agree with this observation; it is crucial that we restore the foundation of truth concerning the gift of prophecy, and, indeed, all spiritual gifts. The flock of Christ must be fed the true word of God, and be nurtured in truth to be able to avoid the corrupt, identify the counterfeit, and mature in the true anointing of spiritual gifts including the prophetic gift.

It is my absolute conviction that we must 'go back to the drawing board' and re-discover the true reason *why* all may prophesy, rather than major on the minor of *how* we may all prophesy. Answering the question of 'why' we are all able to prophesy will bring the gift of New Testament prophecy firmly into submission to the greatest of all gifts – the gift of Christ Himself. Once the believer is Christ-centred then the gifts will follow suit in proper alignment to the Word of God and the will of God, with abundant, good fruit to the glory of His name!

We ought to view all spiritual gifts through the lens of the Person of Christ and the teaching of Christ. Once we understand who Christ is, His finished work, and who we are in Him then we will be able to grow as His disciples in sonship, in character, in servanthood, in ministry, in calling, in fruit, and in gifting including the gift of prophecy. The New Testament matrix of prophecy centred in Christ is glorious and powerful!

I want to re-assure all my readers that this book is not designed to destroy the credibility of the true prophetic, yet at the same time I do advocate that the modern day church must address some glaring issues within the realms of understanding and operating in the prophetic, but that is not the specific focus of my writing on this occasion.

In the last 2.5 years alone, myself, my fellow apostle and our team have trained more than 6,000 leaders and believers in East Africa (albeit our reach is global). In our time with them we teach on Christ and His Kingdom, and we have discovered they desperately need this teaching foundation. So many of them and the churches they lead have been preyed upon by false teachers and false prophets. They did not all have the foundational doctrine to withstand such onslaughts. We are thankful to the Lord for the opportunity to share the truth and love in Christ, to serve them, and to bring restoration through the Word, the Holy Spirit, and our relationship with them.

"The Prophetic Matrix (in Christ)" is intended to be a practical teaching book using the Scriptures, what I have learned in 27+ years of ministry in churches throughout the nations, my experience as a mentor and discipler, my experience as a founding director and team member of our ministry, and my ministry knowledge as a servant apostle who teaches and preaches the word of God … and occasionally … has dreams, operates in discernment, and prophesies.

I will be sharing teaching from Scripture, ministry experience, and testimonies, and along the way we will examine in much more detail the gift of prophecy, the matrix of prophecy within the New Testament, the role of New Testament prophecy and prophets, and how prophets can work together with apostles and other fivefold ministry gifts. Most importantly we will comprehend the importance of revelation, which Apostle Paul defines separately from prophecy (see 1 Corinthians 14:6). Through this process we will lay a foundation of Scriptural truth and Christological application that will help to bring the church into alignment with God's heart concerning the gift of prophecy. It's supernatural!

The five offices (or ascension gifts) that Apostle Paul speaks of in Ephesians Chapter 4, verse 11, are given for the work of the ministry and to mature the church; our greatest ministry here on earth is to know Christ, and to make Christ known.

On this positive and thought-provoking foundation, let's take a deep dive in the Word together to re-examine old truths, and establish new truth in Christ about the New Testament gift of prophecy and other gifts given by the Holy Spirit. We will consider them in individual and corporate application; as well as in the church and in the marketplace.

Building together with Him and you,

Apostle Catherine Brown,

Founding Director, New Destiny Global Ministries

PART 1 – CHRIST OUR PROPHETIC FOUNDATION

CHAPTER 1 – MOSES AND THE PROPHET TO COME

22 For Moses truly said unto the fathers, A prophet [Christ] shall the Lord your God raise up unto you of your brethren, like unto me; him [Christ] shall ye hear in all things whatsoever he [Christ] shall say unto you. Acts 3:22 (see also Deuteronomy 18:15, 18) [Emphasis mine]

To understand the New Testament gift of prophecy, its purpose, its power, and the role of the New Testament prophet in Christ, we first need to comprehend certain Scriptural truths from the Old Testament, which we will consider briefly in this and the following chapters. I do not intend to present any kind of in-depth study of the Old Testament prophets, because this book is for New Testament believers in Christ, and we are looking at New Testament prophecy. Nonetheless, a foundation from the Old Testament will assist us in understanding the prophetic in the New Testament.

Some questions that you might be asking could include: -

1. What was an Old Testament prophet?
2. What were the main functions of the Old Testament prophets?
3. What was the purpose of Old Testament prophecies?
4. Has the office of the Old Testament prophet ceased to exist?

5. What does it mean that the Old Testament prophets prophesied until John?
6. In what way has Christ fulfilled both the Law and the Prophets?
7. Are there still prophecies and prophets today?
8. Is there a New Testament biblical mandate for prophecy?
9. Is the New Testament prophetic gift the same as in the Old Testament?
10. What is the *matrix** of New Testament Prophecy?
   *matrix means the environment, culture, or conditions in which something is formed.

We are going to consider all these questions and more as we look at Christ and the supernatural gift of prophecy with which He has graced His church. We will do this mostly through the lens of the New Testament, focusing on the Gospels and the book of the Acts of the Apostles.

What was an Old Testament Prophet?

A prophet in the Old Testament was an individual who **received a call from God to be His authorised spokesperson.** The message the prophet received came directly from God, and the prophet HAD TO DELIVER THE VERY WORDS OF GOD.

The Old Testament prophet also operated in a type of mediatory role, whereby the prophet heard from God, and then delivered those words of God to the people. The people of the Old Testament were unable to hear God for themselves, other than on rare occasions. Apostle Peter puts it this way, *²⁰ Above all, you must realize that no prophecy in Scripture ever came from the [Old Testament] prophet's own understanding, ²¹ or from human initiative. No, those [Old Testament] prophets were moved by the Holy Spirit, and they spoke from God. 2 Peter 1:20 NLT* [Emphasis mine]

The Hebrew *nabi,* when considered as an active verb, means "an announcer for God."

Another application of the prophet's role was to receive revelation. The Hebrew *hozeh* means "to see a vision" or "to have a vision."

What were the main functions of the Old Testament prophets?

We can identify three principal areas in which the Old Testament prophets operated:

1. Teaching the people of God;
2. Judging/warning/calling to repentance the people of God, and other nations;
3. Foretelling – primarily about the coming Messiah, Christ the Son of God.

The Example of Moses

Although Moses was called a prophet, God appointed his brother Aaron to be his spokesperson/prophet because of Moses' stammer (see Exodus Chapter 7). In fact, God told Moses to put words in his brother's mouth that the Lord

Himself would give to Moses, so that Aaron could speak to the people on behalf of Moses; Moses was to be a mediator for his brother before God (Exodus 4:15-16). Moses' primary calling was as a leader, and a deliverer of the nation of Israel. He was a type, or foreshadow of Christ the Messiah yet to come. Moses was to deliver one people, the Israelites; Christ would deliver all humanity.

- Moses was summoned/called by God,
- Moses received the Law of God;
- Moses taught the people of God how to obey the Law of God,
- Moses functioned as a judge for the people of God;
- Moses interceded for the people of God,
- Moses operated in a mediatory role for the people of God,
- Moses was able to foretell the future (concerning the Prophet [Messiah] to come).

Summoned/Called by God

⁴ And when the LORD saw that he turned aside to see, God called unto him out of the midst of the bush, and said, Moses, Moses. And he said, Here am I. Exodus 3

The angel of the Lord appeared to Moses in the burning bush, which had not been consumed by the holy fire, and called Moses into service to the Lord during that encounter.

Received the Law

²² And the L᎐ᴏʀᴅ said unto Moses, Thus thou shalt say unto the children of Israel, Ye have seen that I have talked with you from heaven. Exodus 20

Moses received the Law (the Ten Commandments) on Mount Sinai (Exodus 20; Deuteronomy 5), and was then instructed by God to instruct the people how to obey God's laws.

Teaching

⁵ "Look, I now teach you these decrees and regulations just as the L᎐ᴏʀᴅ my God commanded me, so that you may obey them in the land you are about to enter and occupy. Deuteronomy 4:5 NLT

The prophet of God was not only to be an oracle for God, but also to teach the people how to understand and apply the revelation to their daily lives that the prophet had received from God, on behalf of the people.

Judging/Warning

¹⁶ When they have a matter, they come unto me; and I judge between one and another, and I do make them know the statutes of God, and his laws. Exodus 18:16 KJV

There were times when Moses would intercede for the people of God, and even occasions when his fervent intercession literally saved the lives of many thousands of them – especially when God was judging the nation of Israel for their rebellion, sin, and hard-heartedness against Him.

Interceding for the nation

An example of Moses' profound, priestly intercession for the people to save them from judgement was seen during the rebellion of Korah, when God was about to send judgement on the entire people.

[20] And the LORD spake unto Moses and unto Aaron, saying, [21] Separate yourselves from among this congregation, that I may consume them in a moment. [22] And they fell upon their faces, and said, O God, the God of the spirits of all flesh, shall one man sin, and wilt thou be wroth with all the congregation? [23] And the LORD spake unto Moses, saying, [24] Speak unto the congregation, saying, Get you up from about the tabernacle of Korah, Dathan, and Abiram. Numbers 16 KJV

Mediation

As the leader of God's people Moses acted in a mediatory role. The people could not hear God on their own. They needed Moses to hear from God, and then to tell them. They also needed Moses to come before God for them. Moses was both an apostolic father figure, and at times a general in battle. He loved God with all his heart, and he loved the people of God with the heart of God.

Foretelling

Moses was a forerunner for the Prophet of God to come [which is Christ]. He prophesied and foretold about a Prophet that God would raise up in the future.

The Prophet to come was Christ [Messiah], the Son of God, although neither Moses, nor the people, nor the religious leaders of Jesus' day understood that Christ Jesus was the Prophet spoken of my Moses in whom all the Law and the prophets would be fulfilled.

²² For Moses truly said unto the fathers, A prophet [Christ] shall the Lord your God raise up unto you of your brethren, like unto me; him [Christ] shall ye hear in all things whatsoever he [Christ] shall say unto you. Acts 3:22 KJV (see also Deuteronomy 18:15, 18)

From this brief overview of the role of Moses, we can see that Old Testament prophets had multifunctional roles.

The Purpose of Old Testament Prophecies

We can separate the prophecies of the Old Testament into three main categories:

1. They were given to instruct and to teach the people of God about His ways, His will, and His character.

2. They were given to warn of coming judgement upon God's people (or other nations) and to call them to repentance.

3. **The primary purpose of prophecy in the Old Testament was to prophesy about, and point to, the coming Christ, the Messiah, the Son of God.**

Let's look at just a few examples of Old Testament prophecies that were pointing to Christ the Messiah: -

Genesis 3:15	Born of the seed of a woman	Galatians 4:4
Genesis 12:2-3	Born of the seed of Abraham	Matthew 1:1
Genesis 17:19	Born of the seed of Isaac	Matthew 1:2
Numbers 24:17	Born of the seed of Jacob	Matthew 1:2
Genesis 49:10	Descended from tribe of Judah	Luke 3:33
Isaiah 9:7	Heir to the throne of David	Luke 1:32-33
Daniel 9:25	Time for Jesus' birth	Luke 2:1-2
Isaiah 7:14	Born of a virgin	Luke 1:26-27; 30-31
Micah 5:2	Born in Bethlehem	Luke 2:4-7
Jeremiah 31:15	Slaughter of the innocents	Matthew 2:16-18
Hosea 11:1	Flight to Egypt	Matthew 2:14-15
Isaiah 40:3-5; Malachi 3:1	Preceded by a forerunner	Luke 7:24, 27
Psalm 2:7	Declared the Son of God	Matthew 3:16-17
Isaiah 9:1-2	Galilean ministry	Matthew 4:13-17
Deuteronomy 18:15, 18	The prophet to come	Acts 3:20, 22
Isaiah 61:1-2	Came to heal the broken-hearted	Luke 4:18-19
Isaiah 53:3	Rejected by His own (the Jews)	John 1:11
Psalm 110:4	A priest after the order of Melchizedek	Hebrews 5:5-6
Zechariah 9:9	Triumphal entry	Mark 11:7, 9, 11
Psalm 41:9	Betrayed by a friend	Luke 22:47, 48
Zechariah 11:12-13	Sold for thirty pieces of silver	Matthew 26:15; 27:5-7
Psalm 35:11	Accused by false witnesses	Mark 14:57-58

Isaiah 53:7	Silent to accusations	Mark 15:4, 5
Isaiah 50:6	Spat upon and smitten	Matthew 26:67
Psalm 35:19	Hated without reason	John 15:24, 25
Isaiah 53:5	Vicarious sacrifice	Romans 5:6, 8
Isaiah 53:12	Crucified with transgressors	Mark 15:27, 28
Zechariah 12:10	Hands pierced	John 20:27
Psalm 22:7-8	Scorned and mocked	Luke 23:35
Psalm 69:21	Given vinegar and gall	Matthew 27:34
Psalm 109:4	Prayer for his enemies	Luke 23:34
Psalm 22:18	Soldiers gambled for his coat	Matthew 27:35
Psalm 34:20	No bones broken	John 19:32-33, 36
Zechariah 12:10	Side pierced	John 19:34
Isaiah 53:9	Buried with the rich	Matthew 27:57-60
Psalm 16:10; 49:15	Would rise from the dead	Mark 16:6-7
Psalm 68:18	Would ascend to God's right hand	Mark 16:19

Because the Old Testament prophets were prophesying about Christ, when Christ came He fulfilled their prophecies in His coming: the testimony of Jesus the Son of man, [who is also Christ, the Son of God] is the spirit of prophecy. The King James Version states,

10 And I fell at his feet to worship him. And he said unto me, See thou do it not: I am thy fellowservant, and of thy brethren that have the testimony of Jesus: worship God: <u>for the testimony of Jesus is the spirit of prophecy.</u> Revelation 19 KJV

What is the testimony of Jesus? It is that Jesus is the Christ, the awaited Messiah.

The New Living Translation puts it this way,

¹⁰ Then I fell down at his feet to worship him, but he said, "No, don't worship me. I am a servant of God, just like you and your brothers and sisters who testify about their faith in Jesus. Worship only God. <u>For the essence of prophecy is to give a clear witness for Jesus</u>. [who is the Christ] [Emphasis mine] *NLT*

The New International version,

<u>… For it is the Spirit of prophecy who bears testimony to Jesus</u>. NIV

The essence (or core reason) for prophecy is to give a clear and undeniable witness that Jesus is the Christ – the testimony of Jesus is the spirit of prophecy.

I want us to answer a simple, but direct question - do we see this in our churches today? Do prophets reveal Christ? Do prophecies point to Christ Jesus our Lord? Do they reveal Him? Sadly, not so many prophecies reveal Christ today, but let us also take note - neither do those who preach, or teach always reveal Christ either. We must ask ourselves why this has happened, because the Old Testament prophets were all prophesying about Christ, and after Christ appeared the New Testament prophetic grace reveals Christ throughout the Gospels and the Acts of the Apostles.

At the time when Apostle Peter had gone to the home of Cornelius, He preached Jesus as the Christ, and then made a remarkable statement concerning the prophets of the Old Testament,

⁴³ To him [Christ] give all the prophets witness, that through his name whosoever believeth in him [Christ Jesus] shall receive remission of sins. Acts 10 KJV [Emphasis mine]

The realm of the supernatural gifts embraces the entire range of the prophetic including visions, trances, dreams, interpretation of dreams, foretelling, forthtelling, revelation and much more! We will look at New Testament examples of these, and how we can comprehend the matrix (conditions and environment) in which prophecy flourished in the church of the New Testament.

For now, let's look briefly at the Greek verbs concerning prophecy in the New Testament:

Revelation 602: Greek apokalupsis - Disclosure: - appearing, coming, lighten, manifestation, <u>be revealed, revelation</u>.

Vision 3706: Greek horasis - the art of gazing, i.e. (ext.) an aspect or (intern) an inspired appearance: sight, vision

Consider how different this is from the Hebrew *nabi*, meaning a prophet, an announcer for God. The Old Testament prophets announced on behalf of God the coming of His Son, Christ the Messiah. New Testament prophets are to reveal Christ, and reveal the mind of God.

CHAPTER 2 – PROPHECY FULFILLED IN CHRIST

[19] We have also a more sure word of prophecy; whereunto ye do well that ye take heed, as unto a light that shineth in a dark place, until the day dawn, and the day star arise in your hearts: 2 Peter 1 KJV

In our previous chapter we have looked at numerous examples of Old Testament prophecies that have been fulfilled in and through the life of Christ – by His birth, sacrificial death at Calvary's Cross; His rising again, and His ascension to the right hand of the Father. What does all this mean for the church of today, and the gift of prophecy? Does it mean there are no more prophets or prophecies? Has revelation ceased? No, not at all.

We need to understand how New Testament prophecy is quite different from Old Testament prophecy. Similarly, New Testament prophets are quite different from Old Testament prophets. This matrix is crucial for us to comprehend, or the gift of prophecy will continue to operate under an old covenant/law mindset. To understand this we must turn our attention to the life of Christ.

Using the same basic principles of functionality of Moses and Old Testament prophets, we can now look at their context in Christ:

Whilst Moses was known as a teacher; **Jesus Christ is the greatest Teacher that has ever lived.**

Moses announced God's judgement to His people; **Jesus Christ redeemed mankind from judgement by the Cross, and through His sacrificial atonement we are forgiven and justified before God. At the ends of the Age He will judge the nations** (Matthew 25:31-46).

Moses interceded for one people. **Jesus Christ makes intercession for all,**

³⁴ Who is he that condemneth? It is Christ that died, yea rather, that is risen again, who is even at the right hand of God, who also maketh intercession for us. Romans 8 KJV

Moses was a mediator for one people. **Christ is the Mediator of the new covenant of Grace,** through which humanity is reconciled to God (Hebrews 9:14-15)

Moses was *called* by God, **but Christ was <u>sent</u> by God, to enable us to be sons.**

³ And this is life eternal, that they might know thee the only true God, and Jesus Christ, whom thou hast sent. John 17 KJV

Whilst we have read how Moses was *called* by God, we comprehend that Christ was *sent* by God. Christ, the Word of God [Logos] is God the Son (John 1:1)! God sent His only begotten Son to the world, to save the world through His atoning sacrifice at Calvary (John 3:16).

Moses was faithful as a servant IN God's house. **Christ is faithful as a Son <u>OVER</u> God's house.**

The Bible teaches us that Moses was faithful as a *servant* in God's house, but Christ is faithful *as a son over* all God's house – which is us, His people.

⁵And Moses verily was faithful in all his house, as a servant, for a testimony of those things which were to be spoken after; ⁶But Christ as a son over his own house; whose house are we, if we hold fast the confidence and the rejoicing of the hope firm unto the end. Hebrews 3 KJV

Sons who Serve

There is a world of difference between being called a son, or a servant. A son has an inheritance in his father's house; a servant does not inherit. A son has a position; whereas a servant has a place. A son has privileges because of his relationship with his father; a servant does not. You can be the best servant in the world, and it will not make you a successor in a father's house; yet you can be the worst son in the world, and you will still be legally permitted to inherit and succeed your father. Being a son is the greatest gift of all.

Jesus Christ came as the Son of God, who is also the Servant of all. Let Christ be our example, so that we also serve as sons: called to serve our Lord and Saviour, and His people.

Christ, the Son of God, is seated at the right hand of the Father high above all. Moses was faithful in his day, but he fades in comparison of the glory of Christ as the Son of God, and the Son over God's house. Moses was a

SERVANT IN God's house; Christ is a SON OVER God's house, which means the church, His body, His Bride.

It is crucial for us to understand that **Christ the Son of God, makes us sons of God through His sacrifice,** *[12] But as many as received him,* **to them gave he power to become the sons of God,** *even to them that believe on his name: John 1 KJV*

[4] But when the fulness of the time was come, God sent forth his Son, made of a woman, made under the law, [5] To redeem them that were under the law, **that we might receive the adoption of sons.** *[6] And because ye are sons, God hath sent forth the Spirit of his Son into your hearts, crying, Abba, Father. [7] Wherefore* **thou art no more a servant, but a son; and if a son, then an heir of God through Christ.** *Galatians 4 KJV*

Whilst Moses received the Law of God, the Bible teaches us that **Jesus Christ fulfilled the Law and the Prophets,**

[17] Think not **that I am come to destroy the law, or the prophets: I am not come to destroy, but to fulfil.** *[18] For verily I say unto you, Till heaven and earth pass, one jot or one tittle shall in no wise pass from the law, till all be fulfilled. Matthew 5 KJV*

The Law is fulfilled by Christ's sacrificial death and resurrection on behalf of mankind. He ushered in a new covenant of Grace, and fulfilled every aspect of the Law by His vicarious sacrifice (Romans 10:4). Through Christ we receive imputed righteousness.

- The prophets are fulfilled because Jesus Christ is the testimony of their prophecy (Revelation 19:10).
- The Person that the Old Testament prophets pointed to was CHRIST.
- The divine Purpose of the Old Testament prophets pointing to CHRIST was to REVEAL CHRIST;
- And to be A WITNESS FOR CHRIST.

Because the Old Testament prophets were prophesying about Christ, then when Christ came He fulfilled their prophecies at His coming. Et voila!

CHAPTER 3 - ARE THERE STILL PROPHETS AND PROPHECIES TODAY?

¹⁶ "The Law and the [writings of the] Prophets were proclaimed until John; Luke 16:16a AMP

Are there still prophets and prophecies today? Yes, but it is crucial that we understand that <u>New Testament prophets are entirely different from the Old Testament prophets</u>.

In the Old Testament only the prophets could hear God, BUT NOW we can ALL hear God because Christ has made us sons. In fact, the Bible teaches us that we have become new [spiritual] creatures through Christ (2 Corinthians 5:17). Therefore, we can draw near to our Father in Heaven and hear His Voice. Let's unpack that some more.

The Law and the Prophets were until John

Jesus instructed the people of His day that the Old Testament prophets prophesied UNTIL John: **¹⁶ The law and the prophets were until John:** *since that time the kingdom of God is preached, and every man presseth into it. Luke 16:16 KJV*

NLT puts it in a fascinating way, *¹⁶ "<u>Until</u> John the Baptist, the law of Moses and the messages of the prophets were your guides. <u>But now</u> the Good News of the Kingdom of God is preached, and everyone is eager to get in. NLT*

The Amplified version adds further nuance and assists us in our understanding, *¹⁶ "The Law and the* [writings of the] *Prophets were proclaimed until John; <u>since then</u> the gospel of the kingdom of God has been and continues to be preached, and everyone tries forcefully to go into it.* AMP

'Until' means up to a certain time, or in anticipation of, or while waiting for. The Law (of the first covenant) and the prophets of the Old Testament were until a certain time. Which time? The time of Christ coming to the Earth and taking on a human nature! When Christ was made flesh and made His dwelling amongst us, the invisible God was made visible. God, in Christ, was with us – Emmanuel, God together with us.

Jesus Christ ushered in the new covenant of Grace and fulfilled every aspect of the Law and the Prophets. After the "until" [which is when Christ came to the Earth] there is a new order of things. The Law and the prophets were <u>until</u> John who came as the forerunner for Christ, preaching repentance and declaring when he saw Jesus, *29 The next day John seeth Jesus coming unto him, and saith, <u>Behold the Lamb of God, which taketh away the sin of the world</u>. 30 This is he of whom I said, After me cometh a man which is preferred before me: for he was before me.* John 1 KJV

After John began baptising and declaring the coming of the Messiah, Christ appeared and immediately began to preach the Kingdom message, *17 From that time Jesus began to preach, and to say, Repent: for the kingdom of heaven is at hand.* Matthew 4 KJV

Christ's coming has ushered the whole earth into a new covenant and the dispensation of His grace. He has ushered in the new covenant and His Kingdom rule by His finished work at the Cross. The Old Testament prophets who prophesied of His coming have been fulfilled in Christ. So what now? Does it mean there is no more need of prophecy or prophets? There is still a place for this gift, but it must be Christ-centred to be fruitful and transformative. This is the matrix we are seeking to understand.

Let's remind ourselves of a foundational truth concerning New Testament prophecy: IT IS TO REVEAL CHRIST.

> *... for the testimony of Jesus is the spirit of prophecy. Revelation 19:10 KJV*

The New Living Translation puts it this way:

> *Worship only God. For the essence of prophecy is to give a clear witness for Jesus." NLT*

The Cessation of Old Testament Prophets

Old Testament prophets no longer exist. It is impossible for them to exist because they belonged to the Old Testament era, and to the dispensation of the Law. We are now under a new covenant of Grace through Christ, who has fulfilled the Law and the Prophets. Apostle John writes of Christ,

*¹⁴ And **the Word was made flesh, and dwelt among us**, (and we beheld his glory, the glory as of the only begotten of the Father,) full of grace and truth. ¹⁵ John bare witness of him, and cried, saying, This was he of whom I spake, He that cometh after me is preferred before me: for he was before me. ¹⁶ And of his fulness have all we received, and grace for grace. ¹⁷ For the law was given by Moses, but grace and truth came by Jesus Christ. ¹⁸ No man hath seen God at any time, the only begotten Son, which is in the bosom of the Father, he hath declared him. John 1 KJV*

Now do not panic! We are about to see how the ending of one dispensation of the prophets of the Old Testament **has now transitioned through Christ into the New Testament ascension gift of prophecy** …

CHAPTER 4 – THE MINISTRY OF CHRIST AND THE PROPHETIC

¹⁹ The woman saith unto him, Sir, I perceive that thou art a prophet. John 4 KJV

Our Lord Jesus Christ has innumerable titles: Son of God; Son of Man; Word of God; Lord of Lords; King of Kings; Master; Teacher; Lamb of God; High Priest; Apostle; Prophet, being just a handful of them.

One of the titles ascribed to Jesus is that of Prophet; many times the people thought He was merely (or *only*) a prophet. Such instances in the New Testament include:

- The people of Caesarea, and even the disciples themselves, until the Father spoke to Simon Peter about His Son, revealing Him as the very Christ, the Son of God (Matthew 16:13-20).
- The woman of Samaria (John 4:19), until she realised Jesus was more than a Jew; more than a Prophet, and that He was indeed the long awaited Messiah: Christ, the Son of God.

Christ is more than a Prophet!

In our churches today so many people *only* know Jesus as a Prophet. They really have no idea that He is the Son of the Living God, and what that means for them as sons of God, born again into Christ's Kingdom. Understanding who Christ is requires a spiritual revelation. The Father enabled Simon Peter to understand that Christ is the Son of the Living God; Jesus Himself helped the Samaritan woman to come to the knowledge of who He truly is as Christ. Likewise, today it is not our flesh and our blood that will help us to see this truth of paramount importance. The Word and the Spirit of God will enable us to comprehend Christ in all His fullness. The Mystery of Christ must be revealed. Unfortunately in our day, the church is often more interested with every other kind of spiritual mystery, besides that of Christ.

When Jesus was born there were numerous people who prophesied at His birth. The people who prophesied over Christ at (and/or near) the time of His birth include:

- Elizabeth who prophesied over her cousin Mary, the mother of Jesus, when she came to visit her at the time when they were both pregnant (Luke 1:41-45).
- Mary who prophesied concerning the Christ child she was carrying (Luke 1:46-56).
- Zechariah who prophesied concerning his "forerunner" son, John the Baptist (Luke 1:67-80).
- Simeon having been led by the Holy Spirit, had a vision at the temple and then prophesied over the Christ child when Jesus was presented on the eighth day for circumcision, according to the Law of Moses (Luke 2:25-35).
- Anna an elderly prophetess/widow who also prophesied over Christ; this was just after Simeon had done so at the temple (Luke 2:36-38).

Jesus Christ moved in numerous ways in prophetic grace including:

Forthtelling – He told Nathanael how He had seen him under the fig tree, *⁴⁸ Nathanael saith unto him, Whence knowest thou me? Jesus answered and said unto him, Before that Philip called thee, when thou wast under the fig tree,* ***I saw thee.*** *John 1:48 KJV*

<u>**Forthtelling** is when you speak and make known something that has already happened i.e. a past event.</u> So when Jesus Christ spoke to Nathanael, He was speaking [*forthtelling*] of a [recent] past event that He [Christ] had *seen* Nathanael under the fig tree in a vision before they met. The seeing was not a physical sight, but a spiritual sight, i.e. a vision. This was, in part, what caused Nathanael to be so amazed, and to declare Jesus to be the awaited Messiah.

Conversely, by the time they had finished speaking, Jesus had shifted into **foretelling** of how Nathanael would see the angels ascending and descending on the Son of Man.

Telephone Number/Bank Account Information/Underwear

Now I want to ask us a question – why are people so impressed when a visiting "prophet" calls out a person's telephone number in the church service? Please help me to understand, because from where I am standing if you do not know your own phone number when you enter church then you are in trouble, and probably much more in need of pastoral care than the words of a prophet!

Why does it matter if a "prophet" can tell you your bank account information? Why are people impressed instead of being concerned about cyber security? And finally, what kind of motivation exists when a male "prophet" tells a lady in church the colour of underwear she is wearing to church that day?? Why don't people see this is totally wrong, instead of behaving like people with no brain! It is not normal. The only person that is permitted to know the colour of your underwear is you, and your spouse! Top tip – avoid "prophets" who call out the colour of your underwear; I think it is fair to surmise that they are wolves in sheep's clothing!

Yet, this is the level of prophecy that we have in so many of our churches today. Can you imagine? Nowhere in the ministry of Christ, or His disciples do we find ANYONE forthtelling or foretelling information on underwear, telephone numbers, or bank account details. Please church – WAKE UP!

Jesus operated in foretelling (possibly more than any other New Testament minister)!

Foretelling is when we speak of a future event that has not yet happened. Christ told His disciples that the Holy Spirit would guide them into all truth and *show them of things to come* (i.e. future events that have not yet taken place), taking from Christ Himself and revealing to the disciples. This is a beautiful and powerful part of the Holy Spirit's role in our lives, coupled with His role as our Teacher and Comforter (see John 14:15-3; John 16:5-15).

The things which Jesus Christ foretold relate to His death at the Cross, His resurrection, His ascension, and His return in glory at the ends of the Age to judge the quick and the dead, and reward His own. Of course, there were so many, many prophets who prophesied of these same things in the Old Testament, because of the importance of what they were foretelling about Christ.

Foretelling is for Divine Purpose

Please make a mental note – in the Kingdom of God foretelling is for divine purpose. The foretelling of Christ's death, resurrection, and ascension are of central importance in our Christian faith and doctrine. They demonstrate the power of God, confirm the deity of Jesus Christ and His resurrection, and they are the grounds of hope for all Christian believers.

[21] From that time forth began Jesus to shew unto his disciples, how that he must go unto Jerusalem, and suffer many things of the elders and chief priests and scribes, and be killed, and be raised again the third day. Matthew 16:21 KJV

[Pp Mark 8:31 pp Luke 9:22 See also Matthew 17:9 pp Mark 9:9; Matthew 20:18-19 pp Mark 10:32-34 pp Luke 18:31-33; Matthew 26:32 pp Mark 14:28; John 2:19-21]

Jesus Christ foretold His journey to the Cross,

- In knowing the ass would be tied up ready for His Triumphal entry into Jerusalem, on what we now call Palm Sunday (Matthew 21:2).
- In knowing there would be a room prepared for the Passover meal with His disciples prior to His crucifixion (Luke 22:10-13).
- In His foreknowledge that Judas would betray Him (Matthew 26:21-25).
- In His foreknowledge that Simon Peter would deny Him (John 13:36-38).
- In His foreknowledge of Simon Peter being sifted (the devil had asked permission before this could happen), but because Christ prayed for Him He foreknew that when Simon Peter turned back he would strengthen his brothers in the faith (Luke 22:31-34).
- In His foreknowledge that Lazarus had "fallen asleep," meaning he had physically died, but that the "sleeping" would not be unto death (John 11:4).

The Lord Jesus Christ also foretold events concerning His return at the ends of the Age,

- In His foreknowledge of the signs of the ends of the Age (Matthew 24, 25).
- In His foreknowledge of the time of tribulation (Matthew 24:21-22).

- In His foreknowledge of the way He will return to the earth in His Parousia (2nd coming), (Matthew 24:27-31).
- In His foreknowledge of the times preceding the rapture, and the rapture itself (Matthew 24:36-42).
- In His foreknowledge that only the Father knows the day and hour of His return (Matthew 24:36)

No one knows the day or the hour of Christ's return. That is total Biblical truth ... but there are those [false teachers/prophets/shepherds] who say otherwise.

Ondo, Nigeria – more than 70 believers freed by police from church

In a church in Ondo, Nigeria dozens of believers were freed by police entering the church. The 77 people included men, women, and children. In total the police rescued 26 children, 8 teenagers and 43 adults. The police raid came after a mother complained her children were missing and she thought that they were in the Whole Bible Believers Pentecostal church in the Valentino area of Ondo Town.

Many of the people had been there since February of 2022 because they had been told Jesus was coming back in April. When Jesus did not come in April, the people were told that it would be September! The people were waiting for Christ's Second Coming and had abandoned schools and places of employment, and had been waiting in church for months.

The police were investigating suspected mass abduction and arrested pastor David Anifowose and his deputy; the victims were taken into the care of the authorities. Preliminary investigations reveal it was the assistant pastor Josiah Peter Asumosa who told the members that the return of Christ would happen in April. Source: saharareporters.com/2022/07/02

Makindi, South East Kenya – death of more than 110 believers

An even more tragic report comes from Kenya, in May 2023 when more than 110 innocent children and gullible adult believers died because they were told to fast by their pastor (MacKenzie), who insisted that they would not be acceptable to Christ on His return unless they were fasting. Many died of starvation, including infants and children. Police reports say that some had been brutally beaten, strangled, and even been suffocated to death. Source: Indiatvnews.com/new/world/kenya-starvation-death-church-case-2023-05-02

These situations saddened me beyond words, and made me angry in equal measure. I cannot bear when God's people are abused through erroneous teaching and false pastors/prophets/teachers. Apostolic authority is given to build the church up, and to tear down every imagination and thought that raises itself against the knowledge of Christ Jesus our Lord; this "tearing down" would include heresies that are being taught about Christ's return. The most dangerous heresies are those that contain some truth. The truth is that Christ IS returning; the heresy being taught and/or presented as prophetic foretelling to the church in Ondo, Nigeria and to others is that we will know when He will return. This is not what the Bible teaches at all.

The Second Coming of Christ – Only the Father knows!

Eschatology, the study of the end times, is a complex matter because of the various beliefs held around the interpretation of the events surrounding Christ's return. Depending on a person's view point on rapture, tribulation, millennial reign etc. this will impact how they view the chain of events surrounding the Parousia (the Second Coming of Christ). However, no matter one's eschatological position, we all agree on one thing – CHRIST IS DEFINITELY COMING BACK. Those who are in Christ will be rewarded and spend eternity in His presence; those who are not in Christ will spend eternity separated from His presence as an everlasting punishment (Matthew 25:31-46). Whilst I cannot address such a deep topic in proper overall exegesis here, let me put down one or two foundational thoughts.

Let me simply use the last two recorded statements of the Lord in Acts Chapter 1,

> *⁶When they therefore were come together, they asked of him, saying, Lord, wilt thou at this time restore again the kingdom to Israel?⁷ And he said unto them,* ***It is not for you to know the times or***

the seasons, which the Father hath put in his own power. *⁸ But ye shall receive power, after that the Holy Ghost is come upon you: and ye shall be witnesses unto me both in Jerusalem, and in all Judaea, and in Samaria, and unto the uttermost part of the earth. Acts 1 KJV*

Jesus Christ had risen from the dead, and just prior to His ascension, the apostles were asking Him when He would restore the Kingdom to Israel. This was an end-time question. It is obvious from their question, that they still had not fully understood that the Kingdom was not only for the Jewish people, but for people of all nations. They had previously had in-depth discussions about the signs of the ends of the Age, which included Christ instructing them to be alert and not be deceived (recorded in Matthew 24 and 25). Jesus answered their questions in Acts 1 with two powerful statements that are critical to our understanding about knowing how to view the timing of His Second Coming.

Jesus answered His disciples' question about the end times and the hour of the restoration of the Kingdom by saying what they did NOT need to know. He told them "***It is not for you to know*** the times or the seasons, which the Father hath put in his own power." The context of the "not knowing" is absolutely specific to the time of the return of Christ. Christ meant they (and we) are not going to know the date when He is coming back. The Greek word for power here is *exousia*, which means authority, privilege, strength, and jurisdiction. It is the Father's authority, prerogative, and decision concerning the timing of the return of Christ.

We have the capacity to know many things with the mind of Christ, but this one thing – the day and hour of His return – is known only of the Father. Let that settle in your mind, because the next time a man or woman of God tries to tell you the date of Christ's return you will stand firm in the truth and say, it is not given to us to know the time of Christ's return! Furthermore, if we think Christ is soon coming back ought that not affect how we share the Gospel? Rather than hide us away as the church in Ondo, Nigeria, we should be reaching out in His love, and with His life-saving Word!

The Lord then said, *"8But ye shall receive power after, that the Holy Ghost is come upon you; and ye shall be witnesses unto me both in Jerusalem, and in all Judaea, and in Samaria, and unto the uttermost part of the earth."*

The word for power here is *dunamis*, meaning miracle-working, explosive power! Christ was promising the Holy Spirit would endow them with power to be His witnesses, and make disciples of all nations. This promise is also for the church today! He did not say we will know of the date of His return and then stay in church until it happens. We, the church, will take the message of the Good News of Christ to the nations preaching the Kingdom ... and then the end will come (Matthew 24:14).

False teachers who are saying we must know, and we will know, the day and the hour of Christ's return are contradicting the words of Christ our Lord. It is <u>not</u> given to us to know that date. What we do know is Christ, and we are to make Christ known, not make known the date of His return!

Eat Grass/Give Money/Buy Water and the Keys of the Kingdom

The Lord spoke and foretold of the rise of all manner of false ministers,

- The rise of false Christs (Matthew 24:4-5, 24).
- The rise of false prophets, false teachers, and false miracle workers (Matthew 24:11, 24).

We do not find Jesus or any of His disciples telling people anywhere in Scripture to eat grass, give money to prophets for a prophetic word, or buy anointed water, or rice, or "keys" of the Kingdom from them in church. Let me say that it is not only such "prophets" who are looking to extract enormous amounts of money – there are some very well-known pastors and leaders who will only permit people to enter they office, if they have come bearing an envelope packed with cash!

In the nations in which we minister, myself and my fellow apostle and our team encounter many "false" ministers, though we thank God that we do also meet legitimate, genuine ministers too. However, we encounter abusive shepherds (the type who instruct their flock to eat grass –

literally); false prophets whose only interest is to take as much money and goods from God's people as possible; those who sell water, sell the "keys of David," indeed they sell anything they can! Even they are selling sweets in churches for up to $20 a sweet, claiming that eating the sweet will make life sweet. Seriously?!

When we deliver our leadership training we are on the front lines with bishops, pastors, and leaders, and many times we must "un-do" heretical teaching in our training conferences. These days people just make things up, and call any kind of nonsense their "doctrine;" or they are influenced by, and teach the doctrine of demons (and Paul warned us of this in his charge to his spiritual son Timothy, 1 Timothy 4:1); or they teach their own opinions and call it "doctrine" (Jesus rebuked the scribes and the Pharisees for doing the same thing in in His day, Matthew 15:9). What the church needs is the doctrine of Christ, coupled with a revelation of His Person (as Apostle John taught in his Epistles). This will release all God's power, love, and authority in and through the end time church. It will cause the church global to mature as sons of God, as we make disciples and see transformation in the nations.

Word of Knowledge

Jesus told the Samaritan woman that she had five previous husbands, and her present 'man' was not her husband. (John 4:16-19). This type of prophetic grace is called a **word of knowledge**.

A **word of knowledge** is when the Holy Spirit gives a piece of information to us about another person, and we have no knowledge at all of that before God speaks it to our minds. It might be concerning the person's circumstances; it might be about a sickness they are struggling with. There are many ways in which the Lord can use the word of knowledge.

I recall ministering the Word of God in a meeting some time back and I received a word of knowledge about a man who was going to commit suicide. I shared the word of knowledge, and no one came forward, or responded, but I prayed in the meeting in faith that God would touch the heart of the man for whom the world of knowledge was intended. To be honest I felt a little bit foolish, and I was concerned I might have made a mistake. However, later that evening I received an email from a man who had been in the meeting, thanking me for the word of knowledge. He had been planning to take his life that night after going home from church. I am ever grateful for the Lord in reaching out to this precious soul and keeping him alive.

Returning to John 4 ... after this the Samaritan woman called Jesus a Prophet. He did not end the conversation at this point, but went on to reveal to her that He was Jesus, the Messiah [Christ]. See John 4:25, 26, 29. Even when Jesus operated in the prophetic, He was revealing Christ! Gloriously, when the Samaritan woman understood Him to be the Christ, she left her water pot and ran to the city to tell people and the whole city came to know *that this is indeed the Christ, the Savior of the world (v42b).*

The woman had no message, or real purpose in life until she met Jesus, who revealed to her that He was the Christ, the awaited Messiah. For this woman it was totally transformative. She ran with the message of Christ to her city and the city was turned upside down by the revelation. Christ came to the city, spent a few days there and hundreds, if not thousands, were swept into the Kingdom of God. When Christ is revealed, the Mission becomes our message.

"Knowing"

The Old Testament frequently makes references to God as being the One who knows the heart of a man, and the heart of a matter. Christ, being God's Son, is no different from His Father. They share the same Nature and characteristics. Christ knew (or discerned) the hearts of His followers, those awaiting healing, as well as the hearts and minds of the Pharisees and Sadducees etc. *[4] And Jesus knowing their thoughts said, Wherefore think ye evil in your hearts? Matthew 9 KJV*

We will more fully consider this in Chapter 6. Of course, God is omniscient – He knows everything!

New Testament Prophets

Jesus trained many disciples, including both men and women, and His initial core succession team were the Twelve apostles; in addition to this He had other disciples (including women). We are not told specifically that He raised up any prophets, teachers, evangelists, or pastors, but Apostle Paul's words in Ephesians 4 reveal that the ascension gifts Christ gave to the church (when Christ ascended to His Father) include apostle, prophet, shepherd, evangelist, and teacher (v11), so we understand these five grace gifts (or offices) are still active in today's church by the power of the Holy Spirit. I love how the NLT version states,

11 Now these are the gifts Christ gave to the church: the apostles, the prophets, the evangelists, and the pastors and teachers. 12 Their responsibility is to equip God's people to do his work and build up the church, the body of Christ. Ephesians 4 NLT

Christ Gave the Ascension Gifts to the Church

It is Christ who gave these gifts to the Church. They are the full representation of Christ's leadership graces. The gifts are ASCENSION GIFTS – meaning the Lord Jesus Christ gave them as gifts of leadership to the church at His ascension to the right hand of the Father. The New Testament gift of prophet is mentioned as the second gift by Apostle Paul. We see clearly that Apostle Paul still includes the gift of prophet, and we understand that it is a *TOTALLY DIFFERENT OFFICE than the Old Testament prophet, because it is an ascension gift given by Christ to the Church, in the new dispensation of His grace after this death and resurrection.*

The Corporate Responsibility of the Ascension Gifts to Equip God's People

Additionally, we note that it is the one corporate responsibility (not responsibilities) of the fivefold ascension gifts [or offices], to equip God's people to do His work, and build up the church, which is the Body of Christ. That means we – the apostles, prophets, evangelists, pastors, and teachers - are responsible <u>together</u> to ensure that God's people are positioned, trained, and equipped i.e. discipled, rising in Christ to become a corporate man. That Christ is revealed to and through the church, and that each ascension gift does their part in the process. It is a glorious, and necessary call to oneness in the fivefold.

Apostles lay the foundation of Christ in the life of believers, and build them through teaching and preaching the doctrine of Christ and His Kingdom, and demonstrating Christ's love, wisdom, power, authority, fatherhood and governance; prophets then teach believers how to understand and interpret the will and purpose of God in their lives; pastors act as shepherds revealing the heart of Christ to God's people, and through His people; evangelists equip God's people on how to declare and reveal Christ to the unbeliever, and teachers teach believers on the various doctrines of the Christian faith, especially giving primacy to the doctrine of Christ and His Kingdom.

The equipping and maturing of the saints is not so that the church can be blessed, but so that the blessed church (the ekklesia) can GO and be a blessing, and make disciples and be effective, fruitful, and functional in every sphere of society, most especially including the family, marketplace/business, government, media, education, health, arts, sports, etc.

The Classic Edition of the (AMPC) version describes the role of the New Testament prophet as, *"inspired interpreters of the will and purposes of God,"* see 1 Corinthians 12:29. I like this!

The New Testament prophet is 1) to reveal Christ and 2) teach believers how to understand, and interpret the divine will and purpose of God in their lives. This has both an individual, and a corporate application for believers in the church and in the marketplace.

CHAPTER 5 – NOW GOD HAS SPOKEN THROUGH HIS SON

² And now in these final days, he has spoken to us through his Son. Hebrews 1:2a NLT

We have clearly established through Scripture that Christ came to fulfil the Law and the prophets, and that all the prophets and the Law prophesied until John (Matthew 11:13).

The last book of the Old Testament is attributed to the prophet Malachi. Yet even although John was known as a prophet in the New Testament era, we can still legitimately say that he belonged to the Old Testament prophet type, in as much as the new covenant of Grace was not fulfilled until Christ went to the Cross.

John had a unique message as the forerunner to Christ. We understand that every prophet who has ever lived prophesied <u>until</u> the time of John the Baptist, the forerunner for the Messiah. The Old Testament prophets prophesied that Christ was coming. John prophesied and announced THAT CHRIST WAS HERE!

God has spoken to us by His Son

The writer of Hebrews tell us that God has spoken unto us by His Son.

Long ago God spoke many times and in many ways to our ancestors through the prophets. ² And now in these final days, he has spoken to us through his Son. God promised everything to the Son as an inheritance, and through the Son he created the universe. Hebrews 1:1-2 NLT

What does this mean? In the Old Testament God spoke to His people through a prophet. Mostly He spoke to the prophet, and then the prophet spoke to the leader, and then the leader spoke to the people. Sometimes the prophet spoke directly to God's people. The prophet was a type of mediator, as we have already considered in the life of Moses.

OT MODEL OF HOW GOD SPOKE TO HIS PEOPLE

God   >   Prophet   >   [Father (Leader)]   >   Believer

This is the meaning of *"Long ago God spoke many times and in many ways to our ancestors through the prophets."*

In the Old Testament the people of God needed a prophet to hear God on their behalf, and make known to them His will. That is why the Bible states,

[7] Surely the Lord GOD will do nothing, but he revealeth his secret unto his servants the prophets. Amos 3 KJV

This statement was true in the Old Testament dispensation of the Law and the prophets. God spoke to His prophets to make known His will. However, this is no longer [exclusively] the case, because now Christ has come and God has spoken to us by, and through, His Son.

Remember the Law and the prophets were until John [the Baptist]. Then John announced Christ, and in His coming, Christ announced and inaugurated the Kingdom on earth, and by His sacrificial death and resurrection He fulfilled the Law and the prophets.

The writer of Hebrews changes the entire flow of how we are to understand prophecy, with the second verse of Chapter 1, *² And now in these final days, he has spoken to us through his Son.*

We Can Each Hear God for Ourselves!

We no longer need a prophet to hear the voice of God. We can each hear God for ourselves <u>because we are sons of God through Christ</u>. This is the matrix - the environment, and means by which - the New Testament gift of prophecy should be understood.

This means that Amos 3:7 is fulfilled in and through Christ, which also means that in this regard, that this Scripture is fulfilled and has "expired." It was 100% relevant in its day, but not anymore! In the New Testament ALL may prophesy, and therefore God does not need to wait to only speak to a prophet before He speaks, or acts.

Or another way to put it is like this – since Acts 2:17-18 states that God is pouring out His Spirit on ALL flesh, and everyone, old and young, male, and female can see visions, dream dreams and they shall prophesy …. then every believer is going to hear God prophetically, not only the prophets!

The office of the Old Testament prophet is closed.

What I mean by this statement is that God TODAY can, and does, speak to His children. We DO NOT need to have a prophet to tell us the will of God. Prophets do not have exclusive access to God that other believers do not have. We all have access to God through Christ and may approach the throne of grace boldly (Hebrews 4:16).

Whilst prophets may not have exclusive access to God, they are spiritually attuned to pay close attention to the heart and mind of God, and for that reason may "hear" God ahead of other believers who are not so attuned to His Voice.

NEW TESTAMENT MODEL OF HOW GOD SPEAKS TO HIS PEOPLE

God   >   through Christ   >   By the Holy Spirit >   Believer

Remember the Law and the prophets were <u>until</u> John, <u>then</u> came Christ preaching and demonstrating the Kingdom, and then Christ gave Himself as an atoning sacrifice for mankind's sin. We can categorically state that **the Old Testament office of prophet came to an end in Christ, and the Law was fulfilled by Him. That is because Christ has become the Mediator of the new covenant** ushering the church into a new covenant of Grace, the dispensation of the Kingdom, and our sonship through Christ. Man no longer needs an earthly mediator with

God, since Christ has become the Mediator (Hebrews 9:11-28).

*¹⁴ How much more shall the blood of Christ, who through the eternal Spirit offered himself without spot to God, purge your conscience from dead works to serve the living God? ¹⁵ And **for this cause he [Christ] is the mediator of the new testament, that by means of death, for the redemption of the transgressions that were under the first testament** [covenant], they which are called might receive the promise of eternal inheritance. Hebrews 9 KJV* [Emphasis mine]

We, the born again believers, are all sons of God through Christ. This is the MOST glorious news. We have access to God through Christ. Our lives are hidden with Christ in God. IT IS BECAUSE CHRIST HAS MADE US SONS THAT WE ALL MAY PROPHESY! Wow, now this is a matrix in which we can rejoice!

This is exciting and revelatory news. But some of you might still be struggling with my comments that the Old Testament office of prophet is closed, and we no longer need a prophet to hear God … in part that is because the church has been conditioned to think in such a way; in part it is because we have not fully placed each spiritual gift to be centred in Christ; in part it is because the church globally is still spiritually maturing.

Let me use a personal story as an analogy to support the point. Incidentally, we are not advocating that people no longer need to listen to their pastor – that is an entirely separate matter, and yes, we do need to listen to the counsel of our pastors (which is different from hearing God's voice prophetically for yourself).

Neither are we saying you cannot receive a prophetic word from a trusted New Testament prophet, but we do want everyone to understand that each born again believer can hear God for themselves!

My Dad

When I was a young girl of seventeen and I had just passed my exams at school with flying colours, I went out shopping one day with my Mum. We met a man who was a friend of my Dad, and he chatted to Mum and then turned to me and said, "Your Dad is so proud of you." I did not have a clue what he meant. He went on to say, "He told me you passed all your exams and got great results. Well done!"

Now you would think I would be happy with such a compliment, but the fact was I was not happy, I was totally confused, and a little bit hurt. I did not understand why my Dad had told a stranger what he should have told me personally, because I was his daughter: that he was so proud of me and my academic achievements. If my Dad had told me first (which was the right thing to do), then I would have been happy with the confirmation that I received from my Dad's friend when we met in the supermarket, and not confused, or hurt.

Can you see where I am going with this? We do not need a "stranger" [a prophet] to tell us something that our Father in Heaven can, and will, tell us by Himself because we are His sons! However, God might use a prophet to confirm something that He, as our Heavenly Father, has already communicated to us by His Spirit.

In similar vein, if I want to communicate to any of my biological sons, or my daughter I do not ask a friend (or a stranger) to contact them for me, and tell them I want to meet them, or that I have something important to discuss with them. Because of our relationship I make my own call, or send my own WhatsApp, or voice note message to my children (biological and spiritual). We communicate directly. Then if they meet their Auntie, or a friend of their Mum, and that person tells them something we have already chatted about, then they are not left feeling like we are strangers, or that they need to rely on the word of another to know my heart, or mind. Believers today do not need a prophet to tell us what God can tell us Himself, but God can use prophets to confirm what He has spoken.

Christ has given us total access to our Heavenly Father. God has spoken to us by His Son, and now we are born again we are sons through Christ, we can hear God's Voice for ourselves. Prophets come to encourage, to edify, comfort and to affirm what God has already spoken to His children. Glory to God! This is a way in which we can understand the New Testament gift of prophecy and the role of the New Testament prophet.

CHAPTER 6 – DISCERNMENT, PERCEIVING, AND KNOWING

⁸And God, which knoweth the hearts, bare them witness, giving them the Holy Ghost, even as he did unto us. Acts 15 KJV

One the single most important things we can comprehend about discernment, is that God Himself knows our hearts and minds. He discerns our motivation by His Spirit, and all is laid bare before Him. From the Old Testament to the New Testament, Scripture affirms this truth.

When Samuel the prophet was sent by God to anoint the next king of Israel, Samuel mistook Jesse's eldest son as the one whom God had called, on account of his stature and good looks. God spoke to Samuel and said,

⁶And it came to pass, when they were come, that he looked on Eliab, and said, Surely the Lord's anointed is before him. ⁷But the Lord said unto Samuel, Look not on his countenance, or on the height of his stature; because I have refused him: for the Lord seeth not as man seeth; **for man looketh on the outward appearance, but the Lord looketh on the heart**. *1 Samuel 16 KJV*

Apostle Peter when he was addressing the Council at Jerusalem concerning the issue of the outpouring of the Holy Spirit upon the Gentiles for the first time at the home of Cornelius the Roman centurion, reminded the Council about the truth of God who knows and looks upon our hearts, *⁸And God, which knoweth the hearts, bare them witness, giving them the Holy Ghost, even as he did unto us. Acts 15 KJV*

Because God knows the hearts and minds of all men, those of us who are born again are also able to operate in this gifting of discerning/perceiving/knowing as we carry God's heart and mind.

When God discerns a matter, or a man, He does so in His perfect wisdom. God's discernment provides us with His thoughts and His heart on any given situation that we lift to Him in prayer, and in seeking His counsel, and receiving practical solutions.

The Oxford online dictionary definition for "know" is:

- be aware of through observation, inquiry, or information.
- have developed a relationship with (someone) through meeting and spending time with them; be familiar or friendly with.

God knows everything; and knowing God is everything! If we know Him, then we can hear His voice and know what to do, and what to say, and how to act. Today so many speak of what they "see." My response is: tell me Who you know and what you know through Him, then I might be interested in what you can "see."

Jesus taught that His sheep [that is each believer] know His Voice, *[4] And when he putteth forth his own sheep, he* *goeth before them, and the sheep follow him: **for they know his voice**. John 10*

The first "knowing" is not a discernment of spirits, and running after demons. No. The paramount and critical "knowing" is to know Him, and to have a relationship with Him. *³¹ But these are written, that ye might believe that Jesus is the Christ, the Son of God; and that believing ye might have life through his name. John 20 KJV*

Examples of Discernment/Knowing/Perceiving in the Life of Christ

Jesus Christ operated in a strong gift of discernment/perceiving/knowing the thoughts and motivations of men. Our examples include:

- **Knowing** [1492] their [the scribes] thoughts when He healed the paralytic man (Matthew 9:4; c.f. Luke 5:22 perceived 1921)
- Knowing the source of the revelation as being His Father by which Peter spoke from, when He stated that Christ was the Son of the Living God (Matthew 16:16; c.f. Mark 8:29)
- **Perceiving** [1097] the wickedness of the Pharisees on multiple occasions! (Matthew 22:18)
- Perceiving virtue had gone out of Him, when the woman with the issue of blood touched the hem of His garment, *"immediately knowing [1921] in himself"* (Mark 5:30)

- Jesus perceived the lack of faith of his apostles, *⁸Which when Jesus perceived [1097], he said unto them, O ye of little faith, why reason ye among yourselves, because ye have brought no bread? Matthew 16:8*
- Knowing [1492] the hypocrisy of the Pharisees concerning paying taxes to Caesar (Mark 12:15)
- He perceived the craftiness of the scribes and Pharisees, Luke 20:23 [2657]
- Knowing [1492] the thoughts of the unbelieving people and the religious leaders, when He was casting out a dumb spirit from a man (Luke 11:17)
- God knew the covetous nature of the hearts of the Pharisees (Luke 16:15)
- Jesus – at the time of washing His disciples feet - knowing (1492) [**saw, and was aware**] *that the Father had given all things into his hands, and that he was come from God, and was going back to God* (John 13:3)
- *"Jesus therefore, knowing all things that should come upon him ..."* **foreknew** all things that would come upon Him e.g. His betrayal and His arrest. (John18:4)
- Knowing the spirit by which James and John spoke, *"Ye know not what manner of spirit ye are of."* Luke 9:55 The brothers did not know, but Jesus knew!
- Identifying Judas as His betrayer when He said, *"... one of you shall betray me...,"*and when Judas asked

if it was him then Christ replied, *"... Thou hast said."* (Matthew 26:20-25; c.f. Mark 14:17-25)
- Jesus perceived (1097) [**knew and understood**] that the crowd would come and try to make him king by force – after the multiplication miracle of the loaves and the fishes, *¹⁵ When Jesus therefore perceived that they would come and take him by force, to make him a king, he departed again into a mountain himself alone. John 6*
- The apostles knew it was the Lord at the time Jesus was cooking breakfast on the beach. (John 21:12)

Greek: eido (1492), means to see, to be aware, and to understand.

Greek: ginosko (1097), to "know" (absolutely), in a wide variety of applications: - allow, be aware of, feel, have knowledge, perceive, be resolved, can speak, be sure, understand.

Greek: epiginosko (1921), recognise, become fully acquainted with, to acknowledge.

Greek: katanoeo (2657), to observe fully, behold, consider, discover, perceive.

Acts of the Apostles Knowing/Perceiving/Discerning Examples

There are at least seven documented examples of discerning by the power of the Holy Spirit in the Acts of the Apostles. Let's look at them one by one, and glean wisdom from them.

Apostle Peter, Ananias and Sapphira

The first example in the book of Acts is in Chapter 5, verses 1-11, when Apostle Peter discerns that Ananias and Sapphira have lied to the Holy Spirit.

³ But Peter said, Ananias, why hath Satan filled thine heart to lie to the Holy Ghost, and to keep back part of the price of the land? ⁴ Whiles it remained, was it not thine own? and after it was sold, was it not in thine own power? why hast thou conceived this thing in thine heart? **thou hast not lied unto men, but unto God.**

Peter discerned what Ananias had done, and Ananias dropped down dead after Peter confronted him! About three hours later his wife, Sapphira appeared before Peter. She was completely unaware of what had happened to her husband. When Peter asked her about the land, she also gave a dishonest reply,

⁸ And Peter answered unto her, Tell me whether ye sold the land for so much? And she said, Yea, for so much. ⁹ Then Peter said unto her, **How is it that ye have agreed together to tempt the Spirit of the Lord?** *behold, the feet of them which have buried thy husband are at the door, and shall carry thee out.*

At which point Sapphira dropped down dead just like her husband had done just a few hours beforehand! Great fear of God fell on the church, and there ensued an outpouring of miracles and ongoing salvations (v10-11).

Apostle Peter simply knew [discerned] what the couple had done: they had lied to the Holy Spirit, and they had kept back some of the proceeds from the house sale. **Discernment exposes any lies, or deceit, and wrong motivation of the heart especially where it pertains to lying to the Holy Spirit and/or attempting to cheat God.**

Apostle Peter and Simon [the former] Sorcerer

The second example is in the book of Acts Chapter 8, verses 20-25, when Apostle Peter observes/discerns the heart of Simon [the former] Sorcerer. Simon repents after being rebuked by Peter and convicted by the Holy Spirit; he then asks for prayer.

It was a discernment by Apostle Peter born out of observation of the way in which Simon acted, and a conclusion reached in the way in which Simon spoke asking to purchase the gift of the Holy Spirit. Simon is not alone in those who seek financial gain for spiritual gifting!

Our ministry has seen firsthand how some [false] prophets and [false] teachers are motivated only by financial gain. We have heard countless stories of how gullible believers (and even leaders) have suffered greatly under their ministry, especially in financial losses.

Apostle Paul warned his spiritual son Timothy about such types of "ministers," who were *ever learning but never able to come to a knowledge of the truth.* In other words, they knew nothing, but thought they knew something (2 Timothy 3:7). Paul goes further to call them *men of corrupt minds and reprobate concerning the faith (v8).*

Apostle Paul also spoke to another one of spiritual son's Titus concerning those who opposed sound doctrine, being vain, deceitful, and whose mouths needed to be shut! He said that *they subvert entire households, teaching things which they ought not, for filthy lucre's sake (Titus 1:11)!* In other words they did ministry for financial gain, causing whole families to suffer.

We know Paul was speaking of [false] prophets for in Titus Chapter 1, verse 12 he says, *One of themselves, even a prophet of their own, said, The Cretians are always liars, evil beasts and slow bellies.*

Returning to Apostle Peter and Simon, he said, *23 For I **perceive** that thou art in the gall of bitterness, and in the bond of iniquity.*

The Greek verb for "perceive" is *horao*, which means to stare, to discern clearly (physically or mentally). Peter looked at Simon, and he listened to Simon, and discerned his heart was not right with God. **The gift of discerning/perceiving lays bare the motivation and intention of the heart and mind.**

Apostle Paul and the Crippled Man

The third example is found in Acts of the Apostles, Chapter 14, verses 8-10, when Apostle Paul perceived the crippled man had faith to be healed.

*⁸And there sat a certain man at Lystra, impotent in his feet, being a cripple from his mother's womb, who never had walked: ⁹The same heard Paul speak: who stedfastly beholding him, and **perceiving that he had faith to be healed**, ¹⁰Said with a loud voice, Stand upright on thy feet. And he leaped and walked.*

This Greek used here for "perceiving" – *eido* - means to see, to be aware, and to understand, and this is exactly what Apostle Paul did. He saw the crippled man, and as he looked at him, he was able to "see" i.e. perceive and understand that the man had faith for his own healing.

The "seeing" is by the Spirit of God. **It is a discernment that can identify spiritual matters. It can "see" faith in others; it can "see" the heart of a matter and a man.**

Apostle Peter Addressing the Jerusalem Council

In Acts Chapter 15 we find our fourth example; as we have previously noted, Apostle Peter is addressing the Jerusalem Council on the matter of him visiting Cornelius' home, and the Gentiles receiving the baptism of the Holy Spirit for the first time (after Peter had preached Jesus as the Christ). Peter said,

*⁸And God, **which knoweth* the hearts**, bare them witness, giving them the Holy Ghost, even as he did unto*

us. *⁹And put no difference between us and them, purifying their hearts by faith."*

Greek: kardiognostes (2589) – **a heart knower**: - which knowest the hearts.

Apostle Paul and the Ephesian Elders

Our fifth example of discernment is found in Acts Chapter 20, verse 29, during Apostle Paul's pastoral sermon to the Ephesian elders.

*²⁹ For **I know** this, that after my departing shall grievous wolves enter in among you, not sparing the flock. ³⁰ Also of your own selves shall men arise, speaking perverse things, to draw away disciples after them.*

This is arguably one of Apostle Paul's most glorious pastoral letters! There is so much wisdom that we can glean from the entire letter, but for now let me just comment briefly on the verse that has relevance for our discussion on "knowing," and discernment by the power of the Holy Spirit.

Allow me to address leaders specifically in this example; we all need discernment and especially those of us who are ministers of the Gospel.

Paul could say *"I know this"* because he had a relationship with each one of the Ephesian elders. He was their apostle, and had been present with them at so many times in their lives, and in their ministries. He had taught them publicly and privately, and had invested much in their lives. He knew them because he had oversight over their lives. When a leader has *oversight* over a people, God also gives them *insight*, and *foresight* concerning those entrusted to them.

- He knew them knew them as individuals;
- He knew their various personalities.
- He knew their different spiritual gifting and experience.
- He knew them as leaders under his apostolic/pastoral care.
- He knew them through relationship, and through shared ministerial, and life experiences.
- He knew from his years of experience as a mature apostle, what can happen when apostolic oversight is removed from a flock.

He knew them because God had given him oversight, which means God gave Paul insight about them – on a one to one basis, and also on a corporate basis.

He knew them because having this oversight and insight, God also gave him some possible [prophetic] insight about what would happen when he departed.

He "knew this" i.e. what was going to happen, because as an apostle he understood that when his apostolic presence was removed from the church, then two things would happen:

1) Savage wolves would come in and attack the flock. Christ equates wolves in sheep's clothing to be none other than false prophets! See Matthew 7:15.

2) From amongst their own number men would arise to steal sheep from the flock through false teaching. Christ uses the wolf analogy in John Chapter 10, when He teaches of being the Great Shepherd of His flock, but that wolves are thieves, destroyers, and murderers of God's people.

The Greek for I *"know,"* is the same as our previous example, *eido* – Paul was aware of what was going to happen; he understood all too well what would befall the church after he left. **This application of discernment/knowing enables us to take Holy Spirit led oversight of situations, and speak with clarity, authority, and wisdom into present and future circumstances especially concerning those we are responsible for before the Lord.**

Apostle Paul and the Impending Shipwreck

Our sixth example from the book of Acts is in Chapter 27, verse 10, when Apostle Paul perceives that although the ship will wreck, all on board will survive.

*¹⁰ And said unto them, Sirs, I **perceive** that this voyage will be with hurt and much damage, not only of the lading and ship, but also of our lives. KJV*

Paul's "perceiving" (Greek: *theoreo*), in this instance was a type of **discernment that led to the foretelling of what was to happen to him, and the crew of the ship.**

Thankfully, not long after this, the angel of the Lord appeared to Paul and assured him that neither Paul, nor any of those on the boat would perish, *²⁴ Saying, Fear not, Paul; thou must be brought before Caesar: and, lo, God hath given thee all them that sail with thee.*

Glory to God. Paul's perception of what was going to happen was met by the mercy of God, and he and the crew were delivered safely to the shore, even after the ship was broken to pieces on the rocks, *⁴⁴ And the rest, some on boards, and some on broken pieces of the ship. And so it came to pass, that they escaped all safe to land.*

Apostle Paul Discerns the Division of the Pharisees and Saducees

*⁶ But **when Paul perceived**** that the one part were Saducees, and the other Pharisees, he cried out in the council, Men and brethren, I am a Pharisee, the son of a Pharisee: of the hope and resurrection of the dead I am called in question. Acts 23 KJV*

This is our seventh example in the Acts of the Apostles of perceiving, knowing, and discerning.

When Paul perceived that the religious Council that had united together and were opposing him was comprised of both Pharisees and Sadducees, he took full advantage of that fact – to preach Christ, and to save his own life! Knowing that the Pharisees believed in resurrection, and conversely that the Sadducees did not, Apostle Paul appealed to the Pharisees, by stating he was a son of a Pharisee, *⁷And when he had so said, there arose a dissension between the Pharisees and the Sadducees: and the multitude was divided.⁸ For the Sadducees say that there is no resurrection, neither angel, nor spirit: but the Pharisees confess both.*

This cased the Pharisees to positively align with Paul, and to turn against the Sadducees who did not believe in resurrection, angels, or the Holy Spirit. On the other hand, the Pharisees did, and amid a divided multitude they said, *⁹And there arose a great cry: and the scribes that were of the Pharisees' part arose, and strove, saying, We find no evil in this man: but if a spirit or an angel hath spoken to him, let us not fight against God.*

It really was a genius move by Paul! Although a huge dissension had arisen against him, he used the gift of discernment to save his life. He was quickly ushered from the Council by the chief captain before he was pulled to pieces (v10)! The following night Paul had an encounter with the Lord, who instructed and encouraged His servant. He told him that just as he had testified of Christ in Jerusalem, he must also witness at Rome (v11).

When Paul "perceived" (**Greek: *ginosko*), it **means he had knowledge of, he was sure of, and he was aware of.** This is an interesting aspect of spiritual discernment, and one that literally saved Paul's life. He used it strategically when he was in an extremely dangerous situation. Godly discernment can literally be a lifesaver! Every leader, and every born again believer needs this gift!

My spiritual father makes me laugh when we talk about discernment; he once said to me, "Catherine, God gave me the gift of suspicion." Of course, it was said in jest, but I understood completely what he meant. He is a great man of God, with wonderful wisdom and discernment. He also uses common sense, and years of experience as an apostolic father to pre-empt certain situations in ministry. He does not always take people at face value, and holds back on making any hasty judgements as to a person's character or motivation. I like this. We are not dummies because we are born again!

Apostle Paul makes a similar tongue-in-cheek comment to the church in Corinth when he said, ... *nevertheless being crafty, I caught you with guile. 2 Corinthians 12:16b*

We are commanded to love all, but the Bible does not tell us to trust all – especially not straight away. Oftentimes people have hidden agendas, and their motivation is not what their words are expressing. It does not mean we need to be suspicious per se, just to be cautious and use common sense, along with the gracious, and powerful gift of discernment from God. We can believe for the best and in some ways expect the worse, simply because mankind is fallible. We must choose to love no matter what, and this will assist us (particularly as leaders) to keep going when people let us down either in ministry, business, or in personal relationships.

I have learned to trust my discernment. It is a gift from God that I treasure and has been of immense help to me in life, and in the ministry that has spanned the nations of the earth from UK, Europe, USA, Central America, Africa, Asia, and Australia. To God be all the glory.

PART 2 – THE MATRIX OF THE PROPHETIC IN THE ACTS OF THE APOSTLES

CHAPTER 7 – PROPHECY IN ACTS OF THE APOSTLES

[17]{.sup} And it shall come to pass in the last days, saith God, I will pour out of my Spirit upon all flesh: and your sons and your daughters shall prophesy, and your young men shall see visions, and your old men shall dream dreams: [18]{.sup} And on my servants and on my handmaidens I will pour out in those days of my Spirit; and they shall prophesy: Acts 2 KJV

I am genuinely excited to write this part of the book because I see such profundity, power, and passion in the supernatural prophetic and revelatory realm revealed in the Acts of the Apostles. It is such an eye opener, and in many ways a stark contrast to how the global church operates in the supernatural and prophetic realm in our day! Yet it provides us with a powerful and wonderful blueprint, a pattern to emulate, creating the matrix of operation for all spiritual gifts in Christ, and by the empowering of the Holy Spirit.

Sadly, what we see in many churches today is often a far cry from the original power, purpose, and effect of the prophetic realm of gifting in the New Testament. I want to take us back into the Scriptures, specifically in the Acts of the Apostles, to see just how the supernatural manifested in the New Testament church with particular emphasis in the realm of the prophetic.

We can study, case by case, the matrix [environment, or culture] in which the prophetic developed in the early church. This includes: -

- Prophetic predictive foretelling
- General prophecy to the church
- Dream/Vision in the night
- Visions – these include both "seeing" and "hearing" spiritually.
- Trance
- Encounters with Christ
- Angelic visitation/angelic intervention
- Open Heaven
- Discernment/knowing.

These prophetic and supernatural occurrences were all happening amidst the preaching and teaching of Jesus as the Christ DAILY - in public and in private - with miracles, signs, wonders, salvations, raising of the dead, disciples being struck dead for lying to the Holy Spirit, other non-believers opposing the Gospel being struck blind, sorcerers getting born again, apostles being imprisoned, beaten, whipped, some even martyred, and the church persecuted and scattered as thousands were born again and swept into the Kingdom of God.

New churches were being birthed, miracles were happening daily, the demonised were set free, nobody was in need, churches were being planted, deacons and elders were being appointed and the glorious Gospel of our Lord Jesus Christ was proclaimed with power in Asia, and Europe, and throughout the entire world!

I have put together a Table of the prophetic gift operating in the book of Acts for ease of reference. You can find this in the Appendices at the end of the book.

Predictive Prophetic Foretelling

It might surprise you to note that there are only a handful of instances in the book of Acts where **predictive prophetic foretelling** is recorded, and both examples are attributed to Agabus the prophet, who came from Jerusalem to Antioch with some other prophets.

²⁷And in these days came prophets from Jerusalem unto Antioch. ²⁸And there stood up one of them named Agabus, and signified by the Spirit that there should be great dearth throughout all the world: which came to pass in the days of Claudius Caesar. Acts 11 KJV

The arrival of the prophets at Antioch happened at some point during the twelve months when the Apostles Barnabas and Paul were teaching and establishing the believers and the church in doctrinal truth. I would guess that it would have been nearer the end than the beginning of that year because the prophets' arrival is mentioned in verses 27-28 (after the Scriptures detail that Barnabas and Saul had been teaching the church for an entire year i.e. laying the foundational doctrine of Christ).

²⁵Then departed Barnabas to Tarsus, for to seek Saul: ²⁶And when he had found him, he brought him unto Antioch. And it came to pass, that a whole year they assembled themselves with the church, and taught much people. And the disciples were called Christians first in Antioch. Acts 11 KJV

The second time Agabus is mentioned is in Acts Chapter 21, whilst Paul was in Jerusalem. Agabus takes up Paul's girdle and prophesied that the owner of the girdle would be bound by the Jews at Jerusalem, and would be delivered into the hands of the Gentiles.

¹¹ And when he was come unto us, he took Paul's girdle, and bound his own hands and feet, and said, Thus saith the Holy Ghost, So shall the Jews at Jerusalem bind the man that owneth this girdle, and shall deliver him into the hands of the Gentiles. Acts 21

The disciples of Paul began to weep when they heard these things. Paul told them not to break his heart, for he was ready not only to go bound to Jerusalem, but also to die for Christ! We can see that the content of Agabus' prophecy was accurate, however, the interpretation was a bit off in as much as both the prophet Agabus, and the other believers failed to understand it was the will of God. Nonetheless, Paul fully embraced God's will.

A legitimate prophetic word will NEVER contradict God's will. The person receiving a prophetic word will either resonate with it, or will have a 'red light' response such as

Apostle Paul in the example above. Agabus was not in error concerning what he had prophesied, however his interpretation and application were not on point, and Apostle Paul re-aligned the prophecy interpretatively in line with God's will.

[12]And when we heard these things, both we, and they of that place, besought him not to go up to Jerusalem. [13]Then Paul answered, What mean ye to weep and to break mine heart? for I am ready not to be bound only, but also to die at Jerusalem for the name of the Lord Jesus. [14]And when he would not be persuaded, we ceased, saying, The will of the Lord be done. Acts 21 KJV

Agabus had accurately received the prophecy through the Holy Spirit, but he wandered into emotions/flesh when interpreting the prophecy. Whilst it can be said that prophecy can minister to a person's soul, (mind, will and emotions), nonetheless **we do not prophesy from our souls!** *The origin of true prophecy must be from the Spirit of God not from flesh, or man's will, or from emotion.*

General Prophecy to the Church – Judas and Silas

The first record of more than one **prophet giving "prophetic words" to the church** in the book of Acts is of the prophets Judas and Silas, when they exhort and encourage the congregation of believers at Antioch. It is on this basis that we might perhaps form an apologetic of believers "receiving" prophets and a "word" in a church setting. We read in Acts 15, *[32]And Judas and Silas, being* *prophets also themselves, exhorted the brethren with many words, and confirmed them. ³³And after they had tarried there a space, they were let go in peace from the brethren unto the apostles.*

It is good that we can find a New Testament pattern of prophets encouraging the church in the corporate setting by using their prophetic gift, but can we please note that this was not the only way, or the main way in which prophecy operated in the life of the New Testament church!

I like how the prophets were part of an apostolic team, along with Paul and Barnabas they had gone to the Jerusalem Council, and were returning with the decree of the Council to deliver the epistle to the churches concerning circumcision not being necessary for Gentile [new] believers in Christ.

The prophets Silas and Judas were in a meeting with the church, releasing words of encouragement; the apostles were, *"teaching and preaching the word of the Lord, with many others also,"* (v35) Great team ministry!

The modern day church has become top-heavy in a "bless me" mentality, but as we study the Acts of the Apostles, it is crystal clear this was not the case in the days of the burgeoning New Testament church. We are blessed to be a blessing, not just to be blessed!

Paul's Apostolic Definition of the Purpose of New Testament Prophecy in Church

The Scriptures record that the prophets Judas and Silas *"exhorted"* and *"confirmed"* the believers in church. This is in line with what Apostle Paul taught the church in Corinth concerning the mandate of New Testament prophecy,

³ But <u>one who prophesies strengthens others, encourages them, and comforts them.</u> ⁴ A person who speaks in tongues is strengthened personally, but one who speaks a word of prophecy strengthens the entire church. 1 Corinthians 14 NLT

We note that a person who prophesies in the New Testament context is: -

1. To strengthen others (not weaken them)
2. To encourage others (not discourage them)
3. To comfort others (not cause them to suffer or be in pain).

We have also previously noted that the Amplified version gives us a helpful definition of New Testament prophets as being those who are *"inspired interpreters of the will and purposes of God,"* see 1 Corinthians 12:29 AMPC. The New Testament prophet is to reveal Christ and to teach believers how to understand and interpret the divine will and purpose of God in their lives – individually and corporately; in church and through the church, to the marketplace and beyond.

"Personal Words" Were NOT The Focus of the New Testament Church

There is no other recorded instance of this type of general prophecy in a church setting in the entire book of Acts. The only other mention of a group of people prophesying is in Acts Chapter 19, when Apostle Paul encounters twelve believers (who only knew John's baptism). He preached Christ to them, laid his hands on them, and they became filled with the Holy Spirit and they immediately began to prophesy – albeit we have no clue as to what they prophesied!

This means that personal prophecy was not the focus of the church, although those who were gifted prophetically did strengthen, encourage, and comfort the church from time to time, lifting them up and not tearing them down. Nonetheless, we will yet see how the prophetic gift has a far more potent purpose and effect than simply "bless me."

Prophecy and Evangelism

Apostle Paul finishes this brief description of the purpose of New Testament prophecy by stating that whilst praying in "tongues" strengthens individual believers, the gift of prophecy [when flowing from a pure motivation and by the power of the Holy Spirit] has the potential to strengthen not just one believer, but the entire church. Wow!

Even when a non-believer enters church and hears prophecy, it can result in their worship of God and their personal salvation,[24] *But if all prophesy, and there come in one [into church] that believeth not, or one unlearned, he is convinced of all, he is judged of all:* ^{25} *And thus are the secrets of his heart made manifest; and so falling down on his face he will worship God, and report that God is in you of a truth. 1 Corinthians 14 KJV*

Get Out of the Flesh and Stay in the Spirit

As an apostolic teaching ministry, we fully embrace the power of the Word of God, as Christ is revealed in the power of the Holy Spirit, including every legitimate supernatural expression of Christ and His Kingdom manifestation here on earth – prophecy included. However, we do not ascribe to the inordinate amount of emphasis that is placed on personal prophecy today. It is this over emphasis on the prophetic, and on being personally "blessed" that has given rise to abuse and misuse of the prophetic gift. Corrupt ministers, or at best, those with questionable motivation, wrong teaching, or a lack of teaching about Christ, take full advantage of this "soulish" and immature dimension of prophecy in the church today.

Balance and Priority in the Prophetic

Apostle Paul was writing to the church in Corinth because they were over-emphasising the gift of speaking in tongues, at the expense of any kind of prophetic expression in church gatherings. Over-emphasis on any spiritual gift can cause chaos in our churches!

In the same manner, an over-emphasis on the prophetic can lead to many disillusioned believers lining up to see their pastor, to ask why their "word" has not come to pass. It can cause confusion, frustration, a personal faith crisis, and even anger at God for not fulfilling the "word." It can even result in believers becoming arrogant, because a visiting prophet "promoted" them with their words, and the believer is now convinced they are at a higher place than their spiritual leader/pastor/apostle/bishop, and in their opinion, their leader is remiss in not immediately promoting them, or accelerating their spiritual faith journey.

It is essential to have balance and give primacy to our relationship with Christ, and His word, otherwise Bibles will potentially be replaced by notebooks of "prophetic words" when there is an over-emphasis on the prophetic. The flock will seek the prophet instead of their shepherd; the flock will spend more time on the "words," than in studying God's Word. The flock will become self-centred, and not Christ centred. This is not conjecture. It is what we have experienced in our ministry, and what many other pastors and leaders have also experienced.

Notwithstanding we are instructed not to despise prophecy. The NLT put it this way, *[20] Do not scoff at prophecies, [21] but test everything that is said. Hold on to what is good. 1 Thessalonians 5*

Spiritual Gifts – not Gifts of the Flesh

Like each of the spiritual gifts described in 1 Corinthians 12, **we must comprehend they are SPIRITUAL gifts - not gifts for the flesh, or of the flesh.** When we desire something that is of the flesh, then the spiritual gift can be tainted, or worse still, corrupted by such soulish desires. When we focus on earthly things at the expense of Heavenly matters, we are in danger of going off track.

In a way this is what happened when Agabus prophesied to Paul about being bound. It was not a wicked desire to want to keep the great man of God with them, but nonetheless it was an emotional, and therefore a soulish desire expressed by the believers, rather than the spiritual destiny for Apostle Paul that the prophecy expressed. We bless the Lord that Apostle Paul did not receive the prophetic word through an emotional lens, but through the Spirit of God and could, therefore, discern the true heart and intention of God in both its interpretation, and in its application.

Without the Love of God we are Nothing

In all spiritual matters, especially pertaining to the gifts of the Holy Spirit we are exhorted to follow the way of love. Whilst Apostle Paul encourages believers to desire spiritual gifts, especially the gift of prophecy, he carefully lays the foundation of humility and love, upon which every spiritual gift must operate.

He places the love of God above all gifts, and tells us that even if we have the gift of prophecy, and can understand all mysteries, and all knowledge, and have faith to move mountains – that without love - we are nothing.

Beloved reader, let that sink in deeply. *God's love is crucial to operating in God's gifts,* and even if you are powerfully anointed and greatly gifted – if you do not have God's love – you [and I] – we have nothing! (See 1 Corinthians 12/13).

Paul and the Twelve Believers in Ephesus

Of great interest and import is a variant example of **"general prophecy,"** which we see in the ministry of Apostle Paul in Acts 19. Paul goes to Ephesus and encounters twelve relatively new believers, and he engages in conversation with them asking if they have received the Holy Spirit. It transpires that they have not even heard of the Holy Spirit, and only know of John's water baptism for repentance and remission of sins. Paul preaches Christ to them and replies thus, *⁴Then said Paul, John verily baptized with the baptism of repentance, saying unto the people, that they should believe on him which should come after him, that is, on Christ Jesus. ⁵When they heard this, they were baptized in the name of the Lord Jesus. Acts 19*

They were baptised into the name of the Lord Jesus Christ. Immediately after this, Paul laid his hands on them, *⁶And when Paul had laid his hands upon them, the Holy Ghost came on them; and they spake with tongues, and prophesied. ⁷And all the men were about twelve.*

The Word, the Spirit, and Prophecy

I love this! The Apostle preaches Christ to people that only know about forgiveness of sin, and water baptism through John, but have never known the Spirit of God. When CHRIST IS PREACHED these same twelve men IMMEDIATELY receive the baptism of the Holy Spirit, AND then they begin to prophesy! We do not know what they prophesied, but gloriously they did so AFTER THE WORD HAD BEEN PREACHED TO THEM. Can we see the powerful combination of the Word and then prophecy? Can we acknowledge that Christ preached releases salvation AND gifting?

The Foundation of Prophetic – Christ Must Be Revealed

It is my firm conviction that if/when we separate the word of Christ from the ministry of Christ, then the church ends up with many, many problems. Conversely, the opposite is true: when we preach Christ - the Word from the beginning - then the church is blessed and people get born again into Christ's Kingdom, gloriously set free, and filled with the Spirit of God ... and sometimes prophesy!

The word preached exegetically by Apostle Paul, released the power of the Holy Spirit upon the twelve men in Ephesus, which in turn became a catalyst for them to prophesy. **The correct foundation for the prophetic (and every other spiritual gift) is, and always shall be the revelation of Christ first, then the gifts follow in the** power of the Holy spirit. This is the Kingdom matrix for all spiritual gifts to flow with good fruit.

We Grow Through the Word – Not Through Prophecy

It did not end with the prophetic. The Apostle then entered the synagogue and spoke boldly about the Kingdom of God for about the next three months. After departing from there, *"he separated the disciples,"* and disputed for the following **two years** in the school of Tyrannus. We see that Paul did not abandon the newly anointed believers. He took them with him as his disciples, and they continued to learn and grow in the Word of God. Paul committed to teaching for two whole years. They, and the others, chewed on the meat of the Word of God!

Prophecy is NOT Scripture

Let me challenge us with this statement: **we do not grow and mature as disciples through prophecy; we primarily grow and mature in our faith through knowing Christ and His Word (Scripture).** Whilst some prophetic words may build our faith by revealing the heart and character of God, and/or affirming something God has already spoken to us, it is the Word (Scripture) that is our daily bread, coupled with the Holy Spirit and His glorious Presence. Even Jesus told the devil we need every word that proceeds from the mouth of God when He was being tested in the wilderness! He did not mean every prophetic word; **Christ quoted Scripture to the devil in the wilderness – not prophecy.**

We note that there are some parts of the global church today that seem to think prophecy is equivalent to the Word. I must state this unequivocally - this is not correct. There is no Bible teaching that can support this. <u>Paul taught the Word </u>(he did **not** prophesy the Word) ... *"all they which dwelt in Asia heard the word [meaning Scripture] of the Lord Jesus, both Jews and Greeks."* V10 [Emphasis mine]

We must place the Spirit and the Word, and the revelation of Christ, the Son of God above every other "prophetic word." Somebody say, "Amen."

Philip's Four Daughters

One final example of a **"group" of prophets** we can identify in the book of Acts is given in Acts 21, *⁸And the next day we that were of Paul's company departed, and came unto Caesarea: and we entered into the house of Philip the evangelist, which was one of the seven; and abode with him. ⁹And the same man had four daughters, virgins, which did prophesy.*

It is so interesting to note that there are four daughters, whose biological father is Philip and he is an evangelist, not a prophet. Perhaps we might draw our attention to the power of the two gifts of evangelism and prophecy operating together to win the lost, with the Word being given pre-eminence.

I cannot help but notice that the Scriptures detail each of the four daughters who prophesied were virgins. Not that

I am suggesting virginity is a prerequisite to be able to prophesy in a New Testament context, however, I like the thought of purity that undergirds the prophetic and all other spiritual gifts!

CHAPTER 8 - DREAMS AND VISIONS IN THE NIGHT

^{12} And being warned of God in a dream that they should not return to Herod, they departed into their own country another way. Matthew 2 KJV

Our Lord Jesus Christ is not recorded anywhere in Scripture as having had any dreams or night visions. However, we can identify in the Gospels how others received dreams about Christ the Messiah and other dreams. The former category include: -

The Wise Men

After visiting the newly born Christ the Saviour and worshipping Him, the wise men received a dream warning them not to return to Herod, *^{12} And being warned of God in a dream that they should not return to Herod, they departed into their own country another way. Matthew 2 KJV*

The Flight to Egypt

The angel of the Lord appeared to Joseph in a dream, and warned him to take the baby Jesus and his wife Mary into Egypt because Herod wanted to destroy him. *^{13} And when they were departed, behold, the angel of the Lord appeareth to Joseph in a dream, saying, Arise, and take the young child and his mother, and flee into Egypt, and be thou there until I bring thee word: for Herod will seek the young child to destroy him. Matthew 2 KJV*

Joseph remained there until the death of Herod. This was in fulfilment of the prophecy of Hosea, *^{11}When Israel was* *a child, then I loved him, and called my son out of Egypt.* Hosea 11:1 KJV

Herod Killed the Children

Enraged by the mockery of the wise men, Herod ordered the murder of an untold number of precious baby boys in Bethlehem and the surrounding area. This lasted for a period of two years. God only knows how many innocent children were murdered during that time. This was a fulfilment of Jeremiah's tragic prophesy, *15 Thus saith the LORD; A voice was heard in Ramah, lamentation, and bitter weeping; Rahel weeping for her children refused to be comforted for her children, because they were not.* Jeremiah 31

Joseph was later instructed by an angel of the Lord that Herod was now dead, and that he should return to Israel with his family, *19But when Herod was dead, behold, an angel of the Lord appeareth in a dream to Joseph in Egypt. 20Saying, Arise, and take the young child and his mother, and go into the land of Israel: for they are dead which sought the young child's life. 21And he arose, and took the young child and his mother, and came into the land of Israel.* Matthew 2 KJV

However, when Joseph heard that Archelaus reigned in Judea in the room of his father Herod, Joseph was afraid to go any further. God warned him in a dream and he turned aside into the parts of Galilee (see Matthew 2:22).

Finally, Joseph came and dwelt in Nazareth with the child Jesus the Christ, and his mother Mary, *²³And he came and dwelt in a city called Nazareth: that it might be fulfilled which was spoken by the prophets, He shall be called a Nazarene. Matthew 2 KJV*

Through these examples of dreams in the Gospels we can see distinct reasons **why the dreams were received:**

1. **Of primary importance is that fact that all the above dreams detailed relate to Christ and His Kingdom.** He is the focus.
2. **They were warning dreams given for protection of life** - both human and Divine. Human in the case of the wise men, Joseph, and Mary. Divine in the case of Jesus Christ Himself, whilst He was still a baby.
3. **These dreams did not need to be interpreted**; they spoke for themselves.
4. **The dreams were pin-point accurate in their timing.**
5. **The revelation contained in the dreams required obedience from the dreamer.** The wise men went a different way as instructed. Joseph obeyed.
6. **The dreams were instructional.**
7. **The dreams were a fulfilment of Old Testament prophecy concerning Christ.**

I do not dream so often, but when I do dream, they are mostly "warning" type, or "instructional" type of dreams. They are extremely vivid and self-explanatory. They do not need any interpretation; they simply need to be believed and acted upon according to any instruction I have received in the dream. This is a good rule of thumb for "warning" type of dreams, and is following the same Biblical blue print I have outlined above.

Warning dreams also require prayer! Many times God will give the dream to avert a disaster, or a heartache of some kind whether personal, familial, ministry, church, or business IF prayer and obedience to any divine instruction ensue.

Acts of the Apostles – Two Examples of Dreams and their Amazing Effects

Apostle Peter reiterated prophet Joel's words on the Day of Pentecost, *[17] And it shall come to pass in the last days, saith God, I will pour out of my Spirit upon all flesh: and your sons and your daughters shall prophesy, and your young men shall see visions, <u>and your old men shall dream dreams</u>: Acts 2 KJV*

Despite all this talk of dreaming and prophesying, no one actually prophesied on the day of Pentecost! However, Peter anointed by the Holy Spirit did go on to preach Jesus as the Christ, and three thousand new souls were swept into the Kingdom that very same day!

There are two recorded examples of dreams and night visions that are recorded in the Acts of the Apostles that I would like to look at here. They are of tremendous significance, and we can learn much from them.

The dreams that believers received in Acts caused the Kingdom to advance powerfully. The first example affects the Gospel and an entire continent; the second example we will look at is, at first, personal to the minister, but then has extremely positive impact on an entire city. Both dreams were received by Apostle Paul.

The First Example: Paul and the Man from Macedonia – A Dream for the Body of Christ

Our first recorded example of a dream (or vision in the night) given to a believer in the Acts of the Apostles can be found in Chapter 16,

⁶Now when they had gone throughout Phrygia and the region of Galatia, and were forbidden of the Holy Ghost to preach the word in Asia, ⁷After they were come to Mysia, they assayed to go into Bithynia: but the Spirit suffered them not. ⁸And they passing by Mysia came down to Troas. ⁹<u>And a vision appeared to Paul in the night</u>; There stood a man of Macedonia, and prayed him, saying, Come over into Macedonia, and help us. ¹⁰<u>And after he had seen the vision,</u> immediately we endeavoured to go into Macedonia, <u>assuredly gathering that the Lord had called us for to preach the gospel unto them.</u>

Apostle Paul and his team (Dr Luke, Silas, and the newly circumcised Timothy,) were on their way to Asia. They had a plan. They had a strong team. They had the Message – Christ. But the Bible tells us that the Holy Spirit forbade them from preaching the word in Asia! They tried to go to Bithynia, but the Holy Spirit prevented them. Eventually they stop along the way at Troas, and Paul had a dream, or a *"vision in the night,"* as Dr Luke records. The vision was of a Macedonian man saying, *"Come over into Macedonia, and help us."*

I love the radical way in which Apostle Paul and his team respond IMMEDIATELY, and in UNITY to the revelatory dream.

First, we note their OBEDIENCE TO THE HOLY SPIRIT; they go His way and not their own (previously) planned way, and they are not fearful of getting it wrong, or embracing change along the way. **The dream is directional**.

They did not take days or weeks to pray about the revelation. Their response is IMMEDIATE concerning the revelatory instruction contained in the night vision to go to Macedonia. **The dream is instructional.**

They are in TOTAL ONENESS concerning the revelation that only one of their team (the leader) received. They trusted their apostle, and the prophetic revelation he received in the night dream was confirmed as being from God by the unity of the response. **The dream is believable.**

The believability of the dream, and their trust in their apostolic leader led the team to have a CORPORATE FAITH response concerning the outworking of the revelation. **Their faith response to the dream was confessional.**

MOST IMPORTANT OF ALL THE PURPOSE OF THE DREAM WAS TO TAKE THE GOSPEL OF CHRIST INTO EUROPE! The Holy Spirit sovereignly sent this team into Europe, to preach Christ there for the first time. **THE DREAM WAS MISSIONAL.**

In Philippi, the Apostle Paul and Silas were dragged into the marketplace and brutally beaten, before being thrown into prison. With what they might have thought to be their last night on earth, the two men of God broke into praise to the Lord they loved and served. God answered their sacrificial love and service in a miraculous way by releasing an earthquake that broke open the doors of every prison cell, caused the jailor and his house to be born again, and the economics of the city to be restored in righteousness.

The false (or corrupt prophetic) had held the economics of the city in a vile demonic grip. This was how most people had made their money before Paul and his team arrived. I wonder if it is much different from many of our lead cities today.

Yet, God used an apostolic team, whom He spoke to through prophetic revelation (the dream in the night), who then preached Christ, won converts, delivered the demonised, and caused an invasion of righteousness in the city of Philippi, Macedonia. The city was set free as the word of Christ, the power of Christ and the eruptive effects of the Holy Spirit tore down demonic strongholds and established the strong hold of the Lord. The economic and business capacity of Philippi was totally transformed in righteousness. Wow! Quite an effect of one dream and an obedient team!! May God do it again in our day, and expose and depose all false, corrupt, or manipulative prophets, teachers, or pastors in Christ's mighty name, raising up true apostolic/prophetic teams to transform cities and nations for His glory! Amen.

Sadly, today there are many false prophets/teachers/pastors who are corrupting their prophetic gift and God's people, and God is going to turn their methods, and their places of operation upside down and free His people, in just the same way the Lord turned Philippi upside down through Apostle Paul and his team.

Europe received the Gospel of Christ - through a dream being acted upon in faith! Can I please exhort and encourage us to "dream big" for God and His glory, and the expansion of His Kingdom!

Malawi, the Angel, and the Vice President of Zambia

I recall a few years ago when I was planning a mission trip to Malawi. I was on target with my preparations, when I had a dream in which a huge angel met me at a "check point," the kind you encounter at a border crossing from one country to another. I tried to pass the angel, once, twice, and each time he prevented me from passing. As I endeavoured to pass him for the third time, He pointed in another direction, looked at me, and said, *"Go to Zambia."*

Whilst I was somewhat frustrated by the huge angel that would not let me pass, when I wakened I remembered the dream of Apostle Paul, and I knew immediately that I was to go to Zambia instead of Malawi at that time. My dream was not a warning dream on this occasion; **it was a directional dream; a missional dream loaded with divine purpose.**

Straight away I changed my plans and took a small team to Zambia. I never knew at the beginning of my obedient faith response to the dream that on the second last night of the mission, I would be invited to go and meet and pray for the then Vice President of Zambia, Dr Guy Scott. We subsequently met and ministered to Dr Guy and several others in executive governmental positions, on the day the Holy Spirit opened the way to meet them in the Zambian Parliament buildings.

If I had been afraid, or disobedient, or rigid in my response to my angelic dream encounter, I would never have gone to Zambia, and would not have had the opportunity to minister to, and pray with, the Vice President of Zambia. Just as an aside – we discovered through chatting with him, that he had Scottish ancestry. I smile when I think of how the Holy Spirit orchestrates every single detail when He is planning to encounter humanity. For those of you who do not know me personally, I am Scottish, and my being Scottish helped to open the door of favour to meet with the then Vice President of Zambia.

Dear reader, I exhort you – obey the revelation that comes to you from the Holy Spirit, and trust His leading, and the leaders He has placed around you for such a time a this.

The Second Example: Paul's Dream in Corinth - A Personal Dream

The second recorded dream in the Acts of the Apostles is also one that the Apostle Paul received. It is different from our first example, in that the dream was a *personal dream for the man of God*. However, the personal dream also had a *corporate* effect as we shall discover.

[9]Then spake the Lord to Paul in the night by a vision, Be not afraid, but speak, and hold not thy peace: [10]For I am with thee, and no man shall set on thee to hurt thee: for I have much people in this city. Acts 18 KJV

We might well ask why God felt the need to give such a dream to His servant. The plain fact of the matter is that Paul was afraid, and he had good reason to be more than a little bit anxious. He had almost been stoned to death in Lystra, after the Jews who had rejected his message in Antioch of Pisidan, and Iconium banded together and came to incite the folks in Lystra against him. Paul almost died in that physical assault, yet he got back up and straight away was preaching as soon as he was able. This dream from the Lord was to be another lifesaver!

Apostle Paul was now in the city of Corinth, having spent the initial weeks there living at the home of Priscilla and

Aquila, fellow tent makers. After spending time teaching them about Christ, and when Timothy and Silas returned to Corinth, Paul was pressed in the spirit and testified to the Jews that Jesus was Christ. As a result of his teaching the Jews vehemently rejected his message.

Paul then stayed at the home of Justus (a worshipper of God whose house was right next door to the synagogue). The chief ruler of the synagogue – Crispus – got born again with his whole house, and many of the Corinthians believed and were baptised. It is at this point that God spoke to Paul in the dream we have just read.

The Gospel of Christ was being preached and people were getting born again into the Kingdom and were baptised. Good news right? Yes, and no! Good news for those being born again, but for Paul there was a potential threat to life and limb! Given his near-death experience in Lystra we can at least attempt to understand his position. It is so wonderful that this dream is a dream that God used to encourage His son, Apostle Paul, at a time when he felt fearful, and probably wanted to run far away from Corinth and the then hate filled Jews that rejected his message. Have you ever felt that way? God knows just what we need, at the exact time we need it.

God spoke by revelation, in a vision in the night and comforted and reassured His servant. So what did God say to Paul?

1. **God addressed the fear that Paul was feeling,** *Be not afraid;*

2. **God told him to keep preaching!** *But speak, and hold not thy peace;*
3. **God told Paul He was present and together with him.** Emmanuel means God together with us in Christ. *For I am with thee;* **Paul's dream was an encouraging dream.**
4. Paul was genuinely afraid for his life. God told Paul that no person would lay a finger on him to hurt him, *and no man shall set on thee to hurt thee;* **Paul's dream was a dream from the heart of his Shepherd King, promising protection.**
5. Paul must have felt extremely isolated and alone because **God addressed this with these words of comfort,** *for I have much people in this city.*

The amazing effects of this dream were far more impactful than we might first realise. Albeit the dream was a personal dream for the man of God, it had a knock-on corporate blessing effect for the entire city of Corinth.

The dream brought immediate comfort and reassurance to Paul that God was with Him; by implication, the dream meant he was in the will of God, and in the timing of God.

Paul's personal faith increased because he was able to respond positively to the dream; he did not run away despite wanting to do so before **he received encouragement from God through the dream.**

The dream gave Paul the reassurance that God had many [other] believers in the city, causing Apostle Paul to remain and not run.

Remaining in Corinth allowed him to re-focus on his mission - there are times when the enemy will try to oppress us and make us feel fearful, simply to distract, or derail us from what God has sent us to do, but God can speak a word that will enable us to rise above the oppression and fulfil our Kingdom assignments. Beloved leader or believer please note - no one was chasing or rebuking "demons of delay." The believers trusted God with all their hearts and responded to the Lord, focused on Christ (not on the demonic), and did not give in to enemy intimidation.

The dream gave Paul sustainability for the duration of God's ordained time and divine purpose for him in Corinth.

Apart from the personal benefits that the dream gave to Apostle Paul, there were also **Kingdom benefits to the people and the city!** We read in verse 11, *And he continued there a year and six months, teaching the word of God among them.* **Wow, the dream caused Paul to stay for another 18 months on mission!**

1. **Paul remained in Corinth**, and his apostolic ministry continued to be a tremendous blessing to the people of the city of Corinth.
2. **Paul continued to preach and teach Christ** – there is no greater message for any people, in any city, at any time.
3. **Paul spent a full eighteen months in the city of Corinth** as a direct result of the reassuring dream, and the city was transformed.

4. **Paul's personal faith being strengthened** by the shepherding grace he received through the dream, had a knock-on effect on those he taught and pastored during his time in Corinth.

It was not all plain sailing after the dream however, but the dream gave Paul the strength and faith he needed to remain in Corinth, despite the difficult circumstances surrounding him. The Jews in the city rose again in insurrection against Paul, and of one accord they brought him to the judgement seat, accusing him of persuading others to worship God in a way contrary to their law. However, God had a Master plan and used Gallio – the deputy of Achaia – to speak on Paul's behalf. He refused to try Paul at the judgement seat and drove away the angry mob. Unfortunately, Sosthenes the synagogue ruler, became a replacement for appeasement of the angry mob, who promptly dragged him to the judgement seat and beat him up instead of Apostle Paul!

The Purpose of New Testament Dreams – God's Word, God's Will, God's Way

When we dream it is not primarily to find out who we will marry, or how God will bless us, though the Lord might speak to us in revelation about a future spouse. However, personal gain is not the reason for revelation. We can clearly see from these Biblical examples, that obedience to a <u>dream from God</u> can: -

- Bring a warning to save lives;

- Set our feet on a missional path that will save multitudes and transform nations;
- Set the prisoners free (those to whom we are sent).
- Release God's instructions to us, and God's purpose through us.
- Unify us, and release the power of God in our midst.
- Establish a city in righteousness.
- Bring salvation, healing, and deliverance to an entire city.
- Cause the economy of a city to be restored in God.
- Become a conduit for breakthrough, and for advancing the Gospel of Christ in all the Earth.

On a personal level, a <u>dream from God</u> can,

- Reassure us when we are down, and our faith is low.
- Encourage a lonely leader, or an isolated believer.
- Break the power of fear to release faith.
- Take the plans of the enemy, and turn it around for the glory of God.
- Enable us to hear the Voice of God concerning our own situation, and concerning our call as His sons and servants.
- Destroy the temporary oppression of the devil, and release new faith.
- Inspire us, and reposition us for the love, the glory, and the Word of God to be released in and through us.

- Enable us to overcome and be overcomers in and through Christ Jesus our Lord and Saviour!

We bless the living God for the gift of dreams and night visions from Him. Men and women of God – dream on and dream big with God!

CHAPTER 9 – WHAT IS A TRANCE?

[5] I was in the city of Joppa praying: and in a trance I saw a vision, A certain vessel descend, as it had been a great sheet, let down from heaven by four corners; and it came even to me: Acts 11 KJV

In these days of zombie movies, and a fascination with all things macabre, it is important for us to understand what the Bible means by someone having a trance experience, and differentiate that from any secular, or worldly definition of a "trance-like state." The few people who had trances in the New Testament were not wandering around like zombies! They had been arrested for a brief period of time by the power of the Holy Spirit, and were experiencing an inertia of the body, whilst their spirits and their minds were actively engaged with the revelation the Holy Spirit was pouring into them at that time.

It Does not Mean You Become a Zombie!

The word 'trance' according to the dictionary can mean: a sleep like altered state of consciousness (as of deep hypnosis) usually characterised by partly suspended animation with diminished or absent sensory and motor activity and subsequent lack of recall: a state of profound abstraction or absorption.

Another meaning according to the Oxford online dictionary is, a half conscious state characterised by an absence of response to external stimuli, typically as induced by hypnosis or entered by a medium.

Biblical Definition

The worldly definition is a far cry from the Biblical definition. Believers who had trances were not hypnotised, and were fully conscious. There was no involvement from a corrupt spiritual source, such as a psychic or medium. The only Person causing a believer to enter a trance in the New Testament is the Holy Spirit.

The noun 'trance' is **only used four times in the entire Bible**. There are two examples in the Old Testament and two examples in the New Testament.

In the Old Testament we read in Numbers 24, verses 4 and 16, how Balaam spoke,

⁴ He hath said, which heard the words of God, which saw the vision of the Almighty, **falling into a trance, but having his eyes open:**

¹⁶ He hath said, which heard the words of God, and knew the knowledge of the most High, which saw the vision of the Almighty, **falling into a trance, but having his eyes open***: ¹⁷ I shall see him, but not now: I shall behold him, but not nigh: there shall come a* <u>Star [Christ, the Son of God, and promised Messiah] out of Jacob,</u> *and a Sceptre shall rise out of Israel, and shall smite the corners of Moab, and destroy all the children of Sheth.* Numbers 24 KJV [Emphasis mine].

There is no reference given in the Strong's concordance for the Hebrew noun 'trance.' However, we note the prophetic significance of verse 17 – that a Star [Christ the Son of God, the promised Messiah] shall come out of [the tribe of] Jacob, and His Sceptre of power, love, and authority will rise out of Israel.

Believers do NOT have a Star.

Please understand this does not mean that believers have "stars." Believers do not have a star; this is an erroneous teaching being promulgated by some "pastors" and "prophets" in Africa at this time. Please do not pay a prophet or pastor to "recover your star." It is a heresy.

Apostle Peter's Trance

In the New Testament we read of two separate incidences of a believer falling into a trance. The first example is Apostle Peter when he recounts his revelatory experience, which happened just before the messengers who had been sent from Cornelius arrived at his home.

Peter was explaining to those of the circumcision who were opposing him [as a Jew] for entering the home of a Gentile [Cornelius]. Peter gave a robust response and explained to them as to how God spoke to him about this matter, beginning with his trance,

*⁵ I was in the city of Joppa **praying: and in a trance I saw a vision**, A certain vessel descend, as it had been a great sheet, let down from heaven by four corners; and it came even to me: ⁶ Upon the which when I had fastened mine eyes, I considered, and saw fourfooted beasts of the earth,*

*and wild beasts, and creeping things, and fowls of the air.
⁷ And **I heard a voice saying unto me,** Arise, Peter; slay and eat. ⁸ But I said, Not so, Lord: for nothing common or unclean hath at any time entered into my mouth. ⁹ **But the voice answered me again from heaven,** What God hath cleansed, that call not thou common. ¹⁰ And this was done three times: and all were drawn up again into heaven. ¹¹ And, behold, immediately there were three men already come unto the house where I was, sent from Caesarea unto me. ¹² And **the Spirit bade me go with them, nothing doubting.** Moreover these six brethren accompanied me, and we entered into the man's house: Acts 11*

What can we learn from Peter's trance?

1. He did not go seeking to fall into a trance. **He was not seeking an experience.**
2. **He was in prayer seeking God.** As a **result of his prayer, the Bible describes he was in a trance.**
3. **During the trance he "*saw*" a message** that was given to him three times. **His seeing was spiritual sight, not something physical that he was witnessing.**
4. **The message was addressing Peter's Jewish cultural bias in a way that made it possible for him to understand - through the revelation he received** – that God was not withholding the Gospel from any person, most especially the Gentiles who had not yet received the Holy Spirit, but unknown to Peter were about to be baptised by the Holy Spirit

through Peter going to Cornelius' home and preaching Christ.

5. **God caused a type of Divine intervention, and an unusual revelatory [trance] experience to communicate an essential truth to his servant**, without which Peter would have struggled to enter the home of a Gentile (non-Jew). As a born again believer, Apostle Peter still needed to learn that his identity in Christ meant he no longer was bound by Jewish cultural restraints about whose house he could, or could not enter!
6. **The timing of the trance was exactly linked to the arrival of the messengers from Cornelius,** who arrived at Peter's door just as he was coming out of the trance.
7. **The revelation enabled Peter to go with them and to enter the home of Cornelius.** Whilst culturally it was not permissible for a Jew to enter a Gentile home, the trance had ensured Peter placed his identity as a born again son of God on a Kingdom assignment above any cultural or religious bias.
8. **The Holy Spirit instructed Peter to go with them, without doubting**.

So we can see from beginning to end that Peter's trance and the revelation he "saw" during that time, coupled with the guiding of the Holy Spirit, and his obedience, was the precursor to the Holy Spirit being poured out for the first time amongst non-Jewish people.

⁴⁴ While Peter yet spake these words, the Holy Ghost fell on all them which heard the word. ⁴⁵ And they of the circumcision which believed were astonished, as many as came with Peter, because that on the Gentiles also was poured out the gift of the Holy Ghost. ⁴⁶ For they heard them speak with tongues, and magnify God. Then answered Peter, Acts 10 KJV

The Greek noun noted in the Strong's Concordance for trance is 1611 *ekstasis* from 1839; a displacement of the mind i.e. bewilderment, "ecstasy": - + be amazed, amazement, astonishment, trance.

The Greek clearly shows us that **a trance** as defined by *ekstatis,* is not of the body, but **of the mind**. It **is not an out of body experience, it is when the Holy Spirit takes over a person's mind to communicate an essential spiritual truth.** This process is so all-consuming that the person is utterly unaware of anything else in their physical surroundings.

Since Peter "saw" we might consider this to be the Holy Spirit releasing certain imagery into the man of God's mind. This caused him to be so amazed, and utterly astonished, and he would have seemed to be in a trance like condition – because the Spirit of God had overtaken his mind and was speaking sovereignly to His servant with imagery using his image centre (mind) to communicate.

We have encountered those in the Body of Christ today who continually speak of being in a state of "bliss," and seem only to want to stay in the presence of God without thought of every evangelising or discipling anyone. This was never what the "bliss" of a trance was all about. It was for the purpose of the furtherance of the Gospel, of lives being saved and transformed by the word of God and the love of God. God's love in Christ is not self-seeking, but selfless.

I recall some years ago a young American lady reached out to me and we spoke on the phone. She was "drunk" according to her own words – on the power of the Holy Spirit. She spoke to me of "the bliss" she experienced with the Lord. The purpose of her call was to find someone who could assist her friend, who had been kidnapped in England, was pregnant, and being held against her will, in threat of her life!

Now, I like to laugh as much as the next person – but there is a time and place for sobriety and being serious, and this was definitely such an occasion. I told the young lady to stop laughing, it was not funny! I enquired if she had spoken to her pastor, and she informed me that she had, although he had not acted. I then went about contacting friends in Women's Aid (an organisation that helps women in abusive, dangerous situations here in UK). By God's grace we put a plan in place, and with the help of Women's Aid and the police, the young, pregnant lady was rescued safely a short while later and was able to fly back to USA. Being in the "bliss" is not so that the body of Christ can get "drunk." The bliss of God is to know Christ, and to make Him known; to reach out to the hurting and those suffering in His love and His power. May God help us in our day.

Paul's Trance

17 And it came to pass, that, when I was come again to Jerusalem, **even while I prayed in the temple, I was in a trance**; *18 <u>And saw him saying unto me</u>, Make haste, and get thee quickly out of Jerusalem: for they will not receive thy testimony concerning me. 19 And I said, Lord, they know that I imprisoned and beat in every synagogue them that believed on thee: 20 And when the blood of thy martyr Stephen was shed, I also was standing by, and consenting unto his death, and kept the raiment of them that slew him. 21 And* **he said unto me***, Depart: for I will send thee far hence unto the Gentiles. Acts 22 (see also Acts 9:23-25)*

What can we learn from Paul's trance?

Paul, just like Peter, was speaking about his trance experience some time after he had received it. When Paul spoke of the trance it was before an audience in Jerusalem when he was arrested (Acts 22). When he had the trance it was shortly after his conversion as he had been preaching Christ in the city. The Jews sought to kill him and at that time he was able to escape in a basket down the wall! They were even fasting to ensure their plan to destroy Saul was a success!

1. Just like Peter, **Paul was in prayer seeking God when he had the trance** – he was not seeking an "experience" of God.

2. This posture and practise of prayer caused him to be in a trance.
3. **Paul both *"saw"* and *"heard"* certain important things during the trance.** We are not told what Paul saw except that the Bible records unusually, *"and saw him saying ..."*
4. **The Voice of God spoke to Paul during the trance.**
5. **The trance and the revelation communicated to Paul were of paramount importance**. Whilst Peter's trance message was for the greater good of many; Paul's trance message was twofold. Firstly, it was for his own safety: his physical life was in danger and the Holy Spirit communicated that he had to leave the city straight away. He said, *"Depart."*
6. Secondly, the Holy Spirit said, *for I will send thee far unto the Gentiles.* **This trance contained a commissioning message of such import!** When Paul was encountered by Christ on the road to Damascus and got born again, he received a commission from the Lord to take the Gospel to the Gentiles. With these words Paul had been reminded of his commission to be an apostle to the Gentiles.

Paul happened to be in the temple, whilst Peter was at home. This shows us that God can meet with us at any time, in any place. You do not have to be in a church building to experience the Holy Spirit overtaking your mind in a trance-like way! You can be in your home, or anywhere in between!

Paul was a new believer when he was in a trance; Peter was a well-established leader when he had his trance. This shows us God is truly no respecter of persons, and is happy to speak by this revelatory to means to any believer, whether brand new or mature. The two examples we have studied include both seeing and hearing in a spiritual sense.

Seek His Presence not an "Experience"!

The men of God were not seeking an experience of God, but they did earnestly seek the Presence of the Lord; they were seeking God in prayer. The information downloaded during the trance communicated crucial, Holy Spirit messages to them concerning their own lives, and importantly, the lives of others through the communication of the Gospel of Christ. I am not saying we should not enjoy the presence of God, as He encounters us – not at all. I am simply saying let God be first, not the experience.

God used trance state to cut through any kind of distraction, culture, bias, or circumstance to communicate His will urgently and clearly to believers. In a trance the mind of the believer is totally absorbed by the mind of God and His will.

The trances of the apostles were not so they could boast about spiritual, supernatural experiences. Please take note that only two people in the New Testament are described as receiving a trance. The revelatory messages of the trances received by both Peter and Paul were transformative, Christ centred, and Kingdom focused. They were not given so that the recipients could enter a state of "bliss" or so that they could be experience "ecstasy." They were urgent spiritual, supernatural communications from God to and through His servants. The messages not only changed lives, but saved lives.

CHAPTER 10 - NEW TESTAMENT ENCOUNTERS WITH CHRIST AND WITH ANGELS

³ He saw in a vision evidently about the ninth hour of the day an angel of God coming in to him, and saying unto him, Cornelius. Acts 10 KJV

Have I ever encountered an angel? Yes. Have I ever been encountered by Christ? Yes, amazingly I have when Christ appeared and commissioned me as an apostle in 2007, and I am so blessed beyond words. Whilst my personal encounter with Christ was totally life-changing, let me not speak about these revelations so much. Let's lay a Biblical foundation for encounters of such kind, so that we have a strong Scriptural basis from which to consider them.

We have just finished reading about Apostle Peter's trance in Chapter 9; let's now look at what was happening with Cornelius, because his encounter with an angel was what started the ball rolling in the first place!

Cornelius the Roman Centurion and the Angel

We have three slightly different accounts of what happened, two from Cornelius himself, and one from Peter in retelling the story to the Jews of the circumcision group, who questioned Peter about the incident (we have just finished reading about this).

Firstly, we are introduced to Cornelius and told that he is a devout man, God- fearing with all his household, a generous hearted man who gave to the poor and a man who always prayed, and interestingly he was also a Roman centurion (Acts 10:1-2).

3 He saw in a vision evidently about the ninth hour of the day an angel of God coming in to him, and saying unto him, *Cornelius.* ***4*** *And when he looked on him, he was afraid, and said, What is it, Lord? And he said unto him, Thy prayers and thine alms are come up for a memorial before God.* ***5*** *And now send men to Joppa, and call for one Simon, whose surname is Peter:* ***6*** *He lodgeth with one Simon a tanner, whose house is by the sea side: he shall tell thee what thou oughtest to do.* ***7*** *And when the angel which spake unto Cornelius was departed, he called two of his household servants, and a devout soldier of them that waited on him continually;* ***8*** *And when he had declared all these things unto them, he sent them to Joppa.* Acts 10 KJV

Cornelius was praying around 3.00 p.m. in the afternoon when he had a vision of an angel coming to speak to him. The angel told him that his prayers, and his giving [alms] to the poor had come to the attention of the Lord as a memorial in Heaven. The angel instructed Cornelius to send men to Joppa to find Simon Peter, and to bring him back to his home.

Despite having no idea at all of whom Simon Peter was, Cornelius obeyed the angelic instruction, and immediately sent one of his trusted soldiers, along with two servants to go to the home of Apostle Peter to request him to come with them to the home of Cornelius.

We have just read of Peter in Chapter 9; he was in prayer just before the messenger party from Cornelius arrived at his house, and he went with them because of the instruction and revelation he had received from God in the trance – despite the fact Cornelius is a total stranger to him. When they reached Cornelius' home, Cornelius related to Peter what had happened and using slightly different wording, he gives us even more insight into his supernatural encounter.

30 And Cornelius said, **Four days ago I was fasting until this hour; and at the ninth hour I prayed in my house, and, behold, a man stood before me in bright clothing,** *31 And said, Cornelius, thy prayer is heard, and thine alms are had in remembrance in the sight of God. 32 Send therefore to Joppa, and call hither Simon, whose surname is Peter; he is lodged in the house of one Simon a tanner by the sea side: who, when he cometh, shall speak unto thee. 33 Immediately therefore I sent to thee; and thou hast well done that thou art come. Now therefore are we all here present before God, to hear all things that are commanded thee of God. Acts 10 KJV*

Narrating to Peter, Cornelius reveals that he had been in a time of extended fasting and prayers and a "man" appeared before him. We understand the "man" to be angel of God.

The Apostles' Arrested and Angelic Encounter

Apart from these two instances of encounter, there are several more examples of angelic encounters in the Acts of the Apostles, beginning with Peter and John. As a result of the miraculous healing of the crippled man at the Gate Beautiful, many people had gathered and were amazed, asking by what name this had happened. Apostle Peter lost no time in preaching Jesus as the Christ to the gathered onlookers. Within a brief period of time this news reached the Council at Jerusalem, and they came and arrested the two apostles. It is any wonder the Sadducees and the other religious leaders were stirred. More than 2,000 new believers swelled the number of the burgeoning church in Jerusalem to 5,000, because of the great miracle!

4 And as they spake unto the people, the priests, and the captain of the temple, and the Sadducees, came upon them, ² Being grieved that they taught the people, and preached through Jesus the resurrection from the dead. ³ And they laid hands on them, and put them in hold unto the next day: for it was now eventide. ⁴ Howbeit many of them which heard the word believed; and the number of the men was about five thousand. Acts 4 KJV

Peter preached another powerful sermon when he and John were taken before the Council, leaving no stone unturned to ensure EVERYONE understood that the only reason the man had been healed was because of THE NAME OF JESUS CHRIST. *¹⁰ Be it known unto you all, and to all the people of Israel, that by the name of Jesus Christ of Nazareth, whom ye crucified, whom God raised from the dead, even by him doth this man stand here before you whole.*

Peter passionately preached Jesus as the Christ. It was because of John and Peter's joint boldness that we read the famous lines of verse 13, *[13] Now when they saw the boldness of Peter and John, and perceived that they were unlearned and ignorant men, they marvelled; and they took knowledge of them, that **they had been with Jesus.***

It is not our education, or our social status that gives us a voice; it is the message of Christ that we live, preach, teach, and demonstrate that causes our voices to be heard by men and women from all walks of life in all nations. It is not our power to prophesy that will enable us to be heard, though God might use prophecy as we speak for Christ; it is knowing Christ, and making Him known that will ensure we have a voice, coupled with the anointing of the Holy Spirit.

Power, positions, and status may give opportunities for Kingdom representation to effect transformation in every part of society also, but we must never, ever, reduce the Gospel to whether a person owns land, or has a title, or vast physical wealth, or whether or not they prophesy (or move in any other spiritual gift) – for it is the endless treasure of the message of preaching and teaching Christ that assures we will bring transformation to nations – not our spiritual gift, or the size, or contrarywise the demise of our wallets that are the deciding factor!

The Council threatened Peter and John and told them in no uncertain terms, they were not to continue to speak about the miracle at the Gate Beautiful, or to teach in the name of Jesus. But the apostles told them they must …

speak the things which we have seen and heard. The people outside were glorifying God for the remarkable things that had been done, because the man who had been healed was more than forty years old.

Having been "let go" by the Council, the apostles returned to the company of believers and a great, and powerful prayer meeting ensued. The believers prayed for boldness and the Holy Spirit shook the place where they were assembled and they [all] spoke the word of God with boldness (Acts 4, verses 23-31).

The apostles continued with all the other believers in a life of commonality. With great power the apostles witnessed of the resurrection of the Lord Jesus Christ, and great grace was upon the entire church. Belongings were sold, and resources shared, such that no one was in need.

Acts 5 relates the story of how Ananias and Sapphira lied to the Holy spirit, Peter's discernment of their actions, and the resultant dropping down dead of both one after the other as a consequence!

Many signs and wonders were done by the hands of the apostles, and multitudes were being born again into the Kingdom of God, as Christ was preached. People were saved, healed, and delivered in the glory outpouring. It is at this stage that the entire company of apostles (as far as we know) were arrested! *17 But that it spread no further among the people, let us straitly threaten them, that they speak henceforth to no man in this name. 18 And they called them, and commanded them not to speak at all nor teach in the name of Jesus. Acts 4 KJV*

Jail Break!

God, on the other hand, had other ideas! Time for the first New Testament jail break. *¹⁹ But the angel of the Lord by night opened the prison doors, and brought them forth, and said, ²⁰ Go, stand and speak in the temple to the people all the words of this life. Acts 5:19-20 KJV*

So the apostles were being set free by the angel of the Lord from the prison cells in which they had thrown because ... they had preached Christ ... and as a result ... multitudes got born again ... miracles happened ... people got healed ... the demonised were delivered, and people were totally blessed! Angels assisted the apostles, and all the believers, and those who were receiving salvation.

The supernatural power and love of God was exploding throughout Jerusalem because a handful of people who loved Christ, preached His name uncompromisingly and the church prayed, and no one was afraid to stand up for Jesus. Can we have such a company in the earth today? They were witnessing for Christ, and Heaven backed them up and a glory explosion was happening all around them ... and they got arrested ... again ... and the angel of the Lord led them out of the prison doors and told them to go back and stand before the people in the temple and preach all the words of this life. And they obeyed.

The church was not preaching angels; the church was preaching and teaching Jesus as the Christ, and angels were sent to assist those who were receiving salvation, and to help the apostles and the church when they were in need or danger.

Prison Ministry

I have never been a prisoner, but I have been in countless prisons – in Scotland, in USA, in Africa and in the Philippines. I have seen God do many miraculous works in those prisons with the broken and the bruised, with the defiant and the defeated alike. We have witnessed salvations, miracle healings and once I even baptised more than twenty believers with one small bottle of water, but I must confess that I have never seen the angel of the Lord break any one of jail ... yet ... but I have witnessed the presence and power of God break out in prisons!

Once we were in a youth prison in Uganda, and a young teenage male got his hearing restored as I was preaching the Gospel (he was completely deaf prior to the healing miracle). No one touched him except God Himself! The young lad was so excited he started doing back flips, and within minutes everyone knew what had happened and the jail exploded with salvations, signs and wonders as young people got born again, and filled with the Holy Spirit. Glory to the Lord Jesus Christ whom we serve!

Now back to the Acts of the Apostles ... What a wonder that the angel released the apostles from prison! But we do not hear about them witnessing about how they saw the angel, or even about how they had suffered, or that they had been arrested. They just go back and keep speaking about Christ. I am not saying you cannot talk about angels, but give Christ His proper place and priority – He is the One angels worship, as we also worship and adore Him.

When the High Priest found out they were not in the prison any more, they despatched the captain with officers to bring them back. The High Priest was furious and questioned them as to why they were still teaching in His Name, and why they had filled Jerusalem with the doctrine of Christ (verse 28). Peter stood amongst the other apostles and answered they had to obey God and not men. He preached up a storm, and the religious leaders were cut to the heart. God used Gamaliel, a doctor of the law, to speak on behalf of the apostles and they departed from the presence of the Council, rejoicing that they were counted worthy of suffering for the sake of His name. Wow!

Apostle Peter and the Angel of the Lord who set him free from prison.

Apostle Peter was also set free from jail by the angel of the Lord. At that time Apostle James had been beheaded by Herod, and the church were earnestly praying to God for Peter to be released. Peter did not understand immediately that it was an angel that was setting him free, and thought initially he was seeing a vision. But the angel led him past guards, and through the iron bars, and set the apostle free. This is the God of the impossible that we serve! There is no plan of the enemy, no death, no destruction that can hold up, hold back, or bring down the believer in Christ. God will send help to His own, for His own glory. When we reach the end of our own ability, God steps in and supernaturally demonstrates His great power, glory, and love – whether we understand, or recognise it immediately, or not!

We Do not Have a Guardian Angel

After Peter had been miraculously released from prison through angelic intervention, he went knocking on the door of where the church were gathered to pray. Rhoda was attempting to explain to the church that he was there, knocking on the door. They did not initially believe her, and someone responded and said, *Thou art mad. But she constantly affirmed that it was even so. Then said they, It is his angel (Acts 12:15 KJV).*

This little verse has caused some confusion in the church. People take it to mean that we each have a guardian angel. I personally do not believe this to be so. As far as I am led to understand, it was (and still is) a Jewish belief [only in certain circles] that when a Jew does a mitzvah (observes the laws and commands of God, and shows kindness to others), they are given an angel that serves as a shield and protection for that person. The angel is merely an emissary, and is not revered, or worshipped. Please allow me to state that I have not found anywhere in the New Testament that supports a believer having their own personal guardian angel. Angelic encounters aplenty yes! Personal, guardian angels – no.

Apostle Paul, the Angel, and the Boat about to be Shipwrecked.

Apostle Paul had an angelic encounter on the boat that was shortly to be shipwrecked. The angel delivered a powerful, life-giving message to Paul, who then communicated that to the others in the ship.

*23 For there stood by me this night the angel of God, whose I am, and whom I serve, 24 Saying, Fear not, Paul; thou must be brought before **Caesar: and, lo, God hath given thee all them that sail with thee.** 25 Wherefore, sirs, be of good cheer: for I believe God, that it shall be even as it was told me. 26 Howbeit we must be cast upon a certain island. Acts 27 KJV*

Angels Minister to Jesus Christ

Even Jesus Christ Himself was attended by angels - in the wilderness when He was tested by the devil, *11 Then the devil leaveth him, and, behold, angels came and ministered unto him. Matthew 4 KJV*

And later in the agonies of His intercession in the Garden of Gethsemane, just prior to the Cross, *41 And he was withdrawn from them about a stone's cast, and kneeled down, and prayed, 42 Saying, Father, if thou be willing, remove this cup from me: nevertheless not my will, but thine, be done. 43 And there appeared an angel unto him from heaven, strengthening him. ⁴⁴ And being in an agony he prayed more earnestly: and his sweat was as it were great drops of blood falling down to the ground. Luke 22 KJV*

If angels ministered to Jesus Christ our Lord in His times of need, how much more will God in His kindness send His angels to assist us in our times of deepest sorrow and trial, as well as to those receiving salvation? I remember when my mum was dying in the hospital, how the Lord sent an angel to speak words of comfort to me. I can still recall his words, "Fear not. Peace be with you. Your mum is in God's hands."

As the body of Christ, let's keep our eyes on Christ, and not on our circumstances.

The Angels on our Mission

One of the first time I ever saw angels was when I was with a group of young adults in Scotland, whom I was discipling at the time. We were returning from a mission trip to the central belt of Scotland, and we had been praying and fasting for a week believing God for salvations, and signs, and wonders. I can still recall when one young man Mick shouted out that he could see angels. I parked the car on the roundabout because everyone in the car was going crazy – they could see lots of angels in the dark night sky! There were so many of them. The power from their presence nearly knocked us of our feet. Everyone could see them, and everyone was amazed at God's goodness. The angels were celebrating, and we remembered how the Bible teaches us that they celebrate when even one sinner repents. Glory to God (see Luke 15:10).

These angels followed us all the way home, and once we reached our home town the angels disappeared. I was so excited I burst into my house shouting that night that the angels had come with us all the way home!

All of this to say, I am not saying you cannot speak about your encounter with angels, just let Jesus Christ be all. Give Him the first place in everything. The angels worship Him, just as we do. I may have spoken about those angels at the time, but the thing I am always talking about is not angels … but Christ!

They could not stop talking about Christ Jesus the Lord!

42 And daily in the temple, and in every house, they ceased not to teach and preach Jesus Christ. Acts 5 KJV

They could not stop talking about Christ Jesus the Lord. It does not say they could not stop talking about angels. I could tell you more stories about my encounter with angels, and how God has used them to help me, or to communicate the Gospel. But let me just say I have seen the ministry of those "flames of fire" the Bible calls angels, in my home nation of Scotland, and in other nations of the earth.

They have arrived when I have been on my own, and when I have been with teams. We have joined with the angels in the worship of our beloved Christ. I have been miraculously "assisted" by them in car wrecks, in airports, and in countless other circumstances, but for now let this suffice. Let me just applaud in recognition and wonder, the dedication of the apostles and the early New Testament church to reveal Christ. Come on church! They have set us an example to follow!

CHAPTER 11 – OPEN HEAVEN

⁵⁶And said, Behold, I see the heavens opened, and the Son of man standing on the right hand of God. Acts 7 KJV

Having looked at the manifestation of dreams in the Acts of the Apostles, we now turn our attention to the topic of visions, which include both "seeing" and "hearing" by the power of the Holy Spirit. Whilst the Old Testament differentiates between prophets and seers, I can see no similar separation in the New Testament. Since all may prophesy (according to Peter's declaration on the Day of Pentecost), then all may "hear" and "see!" Some believers do "see" more than others; that is by the grace of God and the gift within them for His glory.

Stephen the Martyr – Stephen's Open Heaven Vision

The first record of a believer in the book of the Acts of the Apostles having a vision, open vision, or falling into a trance is in Acts Chapter 7, when Stephen [the former deacon] is being stoned to death.

Let's back up a little and remind ourselves of Stephen's journey. He was one of those who were waiting on tables in the early days of the church. A problem had arisen between the Hebraic and the Grecian widows, and the apostles had set aside seven men filled with the Holy Spirit and wisdom to serve as the first New Testament deacons, to help manage day to day issues. The apostles laid hands on them (the seven, which included Stephen), and then the apostles returned to prayer, and ministry of the Word (see Acts 6).

Shortly after this there was a great move of God, and the number of disciples in Jerusalem greatly multiplied. The Bible records in Acts Chapter 6, *[8]And Stephen, full of faith and power, did great wonders and miracles among the people.* Even while God was using this relatively inexperienced young man to preach Christ and do great miracles, he was opposed by religious leaders from the synagogues and they disputed with him. But such was the wisdom and grace upon Stephen, they were unable to curtail him. Certain men then accused Stephen of blasphemy and stirred up the people against him, and the elders and the scribes came upon him, and brought him before the Council. False witnesses spoke against Stephen, and the entire time we are told Stephen had the face of an angel! *[15]And all that sat in the council, looking steadfastly on him saw his face as it had been the face of an angel. Acts 6*

The Word THEN the Open Vision

It is at this point Stephen stood up and addressed the High Priest and all who were gathered there. Stephen's sermon is extremely powerful and confrontational in its Christological truth. With the wisdom of the Spirit of God, Stephen spoke from Israel's history all the way to his present day, rebutting every false accusation against him by preaching the truth of God in Christ. His closing statement rocked the Council and caused such an intense reaction, that it led to his martyrdom. The words from Scripture that Stephen preached about Christ preceded his open Heaven vision of Christ.

⁵¹Ye stiffnecked and uncircumcised in heart and ears, ye do always resist the Holy Ghost: as your fathers did, so do ye. ⁵²Which of the prophets have not your fathers persecuted? and they have slain them which shewed before of the coming of the Just One; of whom ye have been now the betrayers and murderers: ⁵³Who have received the law by the disposition of angels, and have not kept it. Acts 7 KJV

Stephen's Open Vision of Christ Jesus

When they heard these things they were cut to the heart and gnashed their teeth against Stephen. But <u>Stephen was not looking at his opposers. Stephen was having an open heaven vision of Christ,</u>

⁵⁵But he, being full of the Holy Ghost, looked up stedfastly into heaven, and saw the glory of God, and Jesus standing on the right hand of God, ⁵⁶And said, Behold, **I see the heavens opened, and the Son of man standing on the right hand of God***. ⁵⁷Then they cried out with a loud voice, and stopped their ears, and ran upon him with one accord, Acts 7 KJV*

Stephen look up steadfastly into Heaven and,

- He saw the glory of God.

- He saw the Heavens opened, and Christ Jesus standing at the right hand of God. Christ stood up for His servant Stephen.

A Vision – "Seeing" beyond the Physical realm into the Spiritual Realm with Eyes of Faith

If everyone had been able to see what Stephen could see, then he would not have needed to tell them what he saw! Stephen was seeing something that was beyond the physical realm. He was seeing beyond the physical realm into the spiritual realm, with eyes of faith. This capacity to see beyond the physical realm into the spiritual realm is how we might simply define a vision. In the Old Testament seers and prophets saw many unusual things including wheels, winged creatures, and much more. In the New Testament believers – beginning with Stephen – see Christ!

The open Heaven vision corroborated the truth of the word that Stephen had preached – that Jesus was the Christ, the Son of God, and the long-awaited Messiah that the Jews had rejected, who was now seated at the right hand of the Father. In the eyes of these religious persecutors there could be no higher blasphemy. In the eyes of God, there could be no greater truth than for his servant Stephen to reveal Christ Jesus, the Son of God/Son of man in all His majestic glory.

Heaven opened because Christ was preached selflessly, courageously, and with the purest of motivations. The servant of God was granted the most exceptional of *"open Heaven visions"*: -

1. **To corroborate the truth that Jesus is the Christ**, that he [Stephen] had just preached to the Council.
2. **To confirm the deity of Christ.**
3. **To confirm the reality of Jesus Christ's ascension in glory to** the right hand of the Father.
4. **To release the glory of God and the atmosphere of Heaven to Earth.**
5. **To release grace to Stephen for the last moments that he would have on Earth as he was being stoned,** before entering the presence of God for all eternity. The manifestation of God's glory took him beyond his physical pain while he was being stoned to death.
6. The glory and open Heaven vision were also **signs for Stephen to know he was about to enter the presence of the Lord**.
7. **To seal Stephen's martyrdom as being permitted by God, and therefore as being part of God's plan for His son Stephen and His entire church.**

We note that Saul stood giving approval to Stephen's death, and that Saul would very soon have his own life-changing encounter with the risen Lord.

Stephen paid the greatest price any disciple of Christ can pay – he gave his life for the sake of His Saviour and Lord, and for the Gospel of the Kingdom. *⁵⁸And cast him out of the city, and stoned him: and the witnesses laid down their clothes at a young man's feet, whose name was Saul.*

⁵⁹And they stoned Stephen, calling upon God, and saying, Lord Jesus, receive my spirit. Acts 7 KJV

I want us to really grasp the sacrificial power and beauty of this "open Heaven vision" of Stephen the martyr. It was not a gimmick, or a trick. It was not for any purpose other than Truth to be preached, and Light be to revealed in the demonic darkness of the antichrist agenda around him.

I genuinely believe that Saul's conversion was made possible (at least in part) by Stephen's mercy-filled prayer, *⁶⁰And he kneeled down, and cried with a loud voice, Lord, lay not this sin to their charge. And when he had said this, he fell asleep. Acts 7 KJV*

Heaven was opened for grace to be given, and mercy to be manifested. Stephen preached the Word, and his spiritual eyes were opened to see Christ at the right hand of God. The Word of God is catalytic in releasing revelation and opening Heaven, and pouring out glory on God's servants.

The Heavens

These days there are some very strange things that are taught about Heaven, and the heavens. Some people mistakenly teach that we should ascend and descend into the heavenly realms willy nilly, usually citing Old Testament Scriptures as a foundation.

One example they use is from Genesis Chapter 28, where we read that Jacob had a dream and saw Heaven opened with angels ascending and descending upon a ladder, but **he [Jacob] did not ascend, or descend.** The purpose of the Lord speaking to Jacob from Heaven at the top of the ladder in Jacob's dream was **to confirm covenant with him, and to reassure Jacob that he was not alone,** for God was with him. Jacob set up a pillar in that place and called it Bethel, meaning "House of God."

In John, Chapter 1, Christ spoke to Nathanael and told him he would see angels ascending and descending upon the Son of man, though **Christ did not teach Nathanael that we would ascend and descend.** *[51] And he saith unto him, Verily, verily, I say unto you, Hereafter ye shall see heaven open, and the angels of God ascending and descending upon the Son of man. KJV*

The **disciples witnessed Christ ascending into Heaven** at the time of His ascension, and were told by the two angels, *[9]And when he had spoken these things, while they beheld, he was taken up; and a cloud received him out of their sight. [10]And while they looked stedfastly toward heaven as he went up, behold, two men stood by them in white apparel; [11]Which also said, Ye men of Galilee, why stand ye gazing up into heaven?* **this same Jesus, which is taken up from you into heaven, shall so come in like manner as ye have seen him go into heaven.** *Acts 1*

The angel did not mean He [Christ] will come and go, come, and go, come, and go. I do not hold a preterist, or partial preterist position, which advocates multiple comings of Christ. I believe He has come once in His incarnation, and will come back once more only at the ends of the Age to judge the quick and the dead at the time of His Second Coming (Parousia). *²⁸ So Christ was once offered to bear the sins of many; and unto them that look for him <u>shall he appear the second time</u> without sin unto salvation. Hebrews 9 KJV*

We are not instructed anywhere in the Bible, either in the Old, or the New Testaments that we are to seek an experience of ascending and descending to Heaven. However, the Bible does teach that at the coming of Christ, we [who are born again] will be lifted into the heavenly realms to meet Christ at His coming, *¹⁷ Then we which are alive and remain shall be caught up together with them in the clouds, to meet the Lord in the air: and so shall we ever be with the Lord. 1 Thessalonians 4 KJV*

What About Third Heaven Encounters?

Does that mean believers will not have encounters in the heavenly realms? No, not necessarily. However neither Jesus, nor the apostles instructed believers to seek to ascend into the heavens, nonetheless there are a few examples. They are exceptions to the "rule" rather than the norm.

Apostle Paul, in his letter to the Corinthian church, describes a third Heaven encounter which he experienced, openly sharing he did not know if what happened to him was in, or out of his body, *² I knew a man in Christ above fourteen years ago, (whether in the body, I cannot tell; or whether out of the body, I cannot tell: God knoweth;) such an one caught up to the third heaven. 2 Corinthians 12* (Please see my book, *"Delivered!"* on further teaching about this encounter, and what Apostle Paul's thorn means).

Apostle John's revelatory experiences in encountering Christ and the many visions and prophecies John received for the church, recorded in the Book of Revelation also show us that it is possible for believers to have supernatural experiences with Christ, which are difficult to articulate with earthly language! Given the extent and complexity of the revelations that Apostle John received, we will leave those for a future study.

Are there any common factors we can identify in these two occurrences the Bible shares with us? Yes. They reveal Christ!

Come Up Higher

John was told to *"Come up higher."* Why? For what purpose? The last chapter of the Bible is called ... The Book of Revelation ... and the first line of the last chapter is ... the Revelation of ... Jesus Christ to His church.

*4 After this I looked, and, behold, **a door was opened in heaven**: and the first voice which I heard was as it were of a trumpet talking with me; which said, Come up hither, and I will shew thee things which must be hereafter. ² And **immediately I was in the spirit**: and, behold, a throne was set in heaven, and one sat on the throne. Revelation 4 KJV*

Apostle John was invited by a voice in Heaven itself to enter. We do not know whose voice it was, whether it was an angel or the Lord Himself, but a voice spoke to John to make invitation, and even before he was able to enter, a door had to open in Heaven for access for the servant of God. I do think since John saw the Lord on His throne, that the Voice was most likely that of Christ Himself but we cannot say conclusively.

John did not try to manipulate going into the heavenly realms. He was invited to do so. This shows it is possible to have open Heaven encounters, but that we are not the ones to orchestrate them, as many seem to be wrongly teaching today.

"In The Spirit"

John said he was *"in the spirit"* immediately. What does it mean? How is it possible to be *"in the spirit?"* It is possible because John was a born again believer. Jesus taught Nicodemus that a man must be born again, *⁵Jesus answered, Verily, verily, I say unto thee, Except a man be born of water and of the Spirit, he cannot enter into the kingdom of God. John 3 KJV*

To be *"in the spirit"* means we must first become spiritual "creatures." The Kingdom of God is a spiritual Kingdom, which affects the natural earth. We are earthly creatures until we are born again into God's [spiritual] Kingdom, at which time we become spiritual creatures (2 Corinthians 5:17) and we have access into the spiritual realm to our

Heavenly Father through Christ, and by the power of the Holy Spirit.

We still have physical bodies, and we still live on physical planet Earth, but our spirits are regenerated by the Holy Spirit when we are converted, and we become brand new through Christ, *⁵ he saved us, not because of the righteous things we had done, but because of his mercy.* **He washed away our sins, giving us a new birth and new life through the Holy Spirit.** *Titus 3* NLT

This is why it is possible for Apostle John to say that he was *"in the spirit."*

Apostle Paul teaches us that we have been rescued from the kingdom of darkness, and that we have been transferred into the Kingdom of God's own dear Son, Christ (Colossians 1:13).

Apostle Paul wrote to the church in Corinth, with words that help us so much to understand that being in Christ makes us *"a new creature,"* and that all the things pertaining to our old life have been taken away and everything is made new!

¹⁷ Therefore ***if any man be in Christ, he is a new [spiritual] creature****: old things are passed away; behold, all things are become new. 2 Corinthians 5:17 KJV* [Emphasis mine]

It is important for us to comprehend that when we are born again we are raised with Christ in heavenly places. By becoming new spiritual "creatures" as Paul wrote, we can have encounters and spiritual experiences that are not confined only to the physical realm. This helps us to comprehend how the apostles' can use phrases such as *"in the spirit,"* and wonder if what happened to them was *"in the body"* or *"out of the body."*

*⁴But God, who is rich in mercy, for his great love wherewith he loved us, ⁵Even when we were dead in sins, hath **quickened us together with Christ,** (by grace ye are saved;) ⁶And hath **raised us up together,** and **made us sit together in heavenly places in Christ Jesus:** ⁷That in the ages to come he might shew the exceeding riches of his grace in his kindness toward us **through Christ Jesus**. ⁸For by grace are ye saved through faith;** and that not of yourselves: it is the gift of God: Ephesians 2 KJV*

- With Christ
- In Christ
- Through Christ

Seated in Heavenly Places – a Spiritual Position in Sonship

Paul says that we are raised up and seated **in** heavenly places because we are in **Christ**. The Strong's Concordance gives us no clue as to the original Greek interpretation of *"heavenly places,"* therefore we must use wisdom and knowledge in Christ to interpret what it means. Being seated in heavenly places is a spiritual position, it is not a physical seat, but a spiritual "seat" [position] in and through Christ, which we occupy. I am making a point about it not being a physical seat because I recently read a prophetic "word" that apparently was describing what this "seat" looks like. Let me reiterate – it is not a seat; it is a spiritual position.

This "position" we occupy is a reference to our sonship, and a result of our sonship. The being *seated* is a reference to our relational and victorious "position" in Christ as sons of God because of being *"quickened,"* meaning *"combined" together with Christ*. We are born again as spiritual creatures with Christ, because of Christ's finished work at the Cross. Being born again means we have access to God and to the spiritual realms through Christ and the Holy Spirit.

Christ has made us to be sons of God, and through Christ we are adopted into God's family. Hallelujah! (see John 1:12; Galatians 4:5-7).

This position in Christ, as sons of God, also means we have authority through Christ. This is because Christ created all things (in Heaven and on Earth, including every spiritual power) and because He is before all things, and all things are in subjection to Him. Consequently, we are above powers and principalities, dominions, and thrones because we are *in Christ*. We are already above every demonic power and ruler! We are already above every circumstance and oppression because we are in Christ. We are already victorious because Christ has won the victory for us!

We do not need to ascend into Heaven to gain victory because we are already victorious [positionally] in Christ, who is in Heaven, and Christ is also in us the hope of glory! Heaven – the presence of God – is in us through Christ.

There is a ministry in USA that is teaching new believers that when they are baptised in water, they are going to ascend into Heaven. This "doctrine" has come as a result of the Hispanic pastor who apparently had an ascension experience when he was water baptised himself. I have no issue with the pastor having a supernatural experience at such a precious time in his life. I do believe the pastor genuinely loves the Lor, and I am not questioning his own personal experience; however, I do not believe the pastor is teaching accurately when he insists that believers "must" have an ascension experience at the time of their water baptism. This is not Biblical.

[16] Let us therefore come boldly unto the throne of grace, that we may obtain mercy, and find grace to help in time of need. Hebrews 4:16 KJV

"Come boldly before the throne of grace" means: -

- Through Christ,
- By the power of the Holy Spirit,
- We have access to the Father,
- And this is a continuous access, and privilege for every believer.

We now have some foundational Scriptural understanding of how it was possible for Apostle John (and for us) to be *"in the spirit,"* and what that means for us today as believers too.

When these men of God talk about their encounters, they major on Christ; they do NOT major on the experience. **Please do not create doctrine out of experience.** We already have our God-given doctrine through Christ's life, teaching, and ministry.

Our ministry was once told by a man who got born again [who used to be involved in the occult and astral travel] that when he participated in this practise (with others), they would see holy fire over believer's homes, and over churches, where prayers were taking place. He told that if that holy fire touched them, they would instantly die (physically). Can you imagine! The prayers of just one born again believer, they were sending holy fire without even knowing, into the spiritual realm that destroys demonically inspired works and messengers! Such is the absolute power and authority of Christ.

CHAPTER 12 - PROPHETIC PREACHING, TEACHING & EVANGELISM

[31]And he said How can I, except some man should guide me? And he desired Philip that he would come up and sit with him. Acts 8 KJV

Prophecy was always meant to be in balance with the Word. One of the greatest expressions of revelation is the illumination of the Scriptures. God is calling His body to engage apostolically and prophetically with His Word.

In 1 Corinthians Chapter 14, verse 6, Apostle Paul mentions four different dynamics in which he speaks to the church:

- **Revelation** (*divine disclosure, uncover, make known*)
- **[Divinely inspired] knowledge** (*have, know, can speak, perceive, be sure, to know absolutely*)
- **Prophecy** (*foretelling, inspired speech, speaking under inspiration*)
- **Doctrine** (*didache – teaching*)

We note that *"revelation"* is in a separate category from *"prophecy."* What could this mean? The Greek interpretation above assists us in comprehending what Apostle Paul meant.

Revelation i.e. divine disclosure can happen when the Holy Spirit illuminates the Word of God, to bring fresh understanding to our minds. Paul was not speaking about foretelling the future, or inspired speech, meaning prophecy; that is in the third category he mentions above. He was speaking about wisdom revealed by the Holy Spirit, shedding light on the Word, and bringing deep, understanding to our minds.

How we long for the Body of Christ to embrace this apostolic and prophetic utterance of the Word of God. That as the Word is studied, meditated upon, prayed through, taught, and preached, the Holy Spirit will magnificently illuminate it and reveal the Mystery that is Christ, and His Kingdom to and through His church!

Philip and the Ethiopian Eunuch

Let me draw our attention to Acts Chapter 8, where we meet Philip preaching Christ in the city of Samaria, due to the scattering that was a direct result of persecution of the church. Philip is a young man, the former deacon, and is at the centre of a Kingdom explosion with salvations, deliverances, and all types of healings occurring. Simon the sorcerer is also converted, and when the apostles hear about what is happening in Samaria, Peter and John come from Jerusalem, to help establish the Kingdom work.

Shortly after this, the Bible details an interesting narrative about Philip. The angel of the Lord appeared to Philip and told him to go south to Gaza from Jerusalem. Philip did as he was bid, and he met a man of Ethiopia, who was a eunuch of great authority under Queen Candace of the

Ethiopians. He oversaw her treasury, and had come to Jerusalem to worship.

The Holy Spirit then spoke to Philip saying, *Go near, and join thyself to this chariot* (v29). As Philip approached the chariot he heard the man reading from the prophet Isaiah, and he asked if he understood what he was reading.

The eunuch replied, *How can I, except some man should guide me? And he desired Philip that he would come up and sit with him.*

The Ethiopian eunuch was reading from Isaiah Chapter 53:7, *⁷He was oppressed, and he was afflicted, yet he opened not his mouth: he is brought as a lamb to the slaughter, and as a sheep before her shearers is dumb, so he openeth not his mouth. KJV*

The man was so eager to understand who the prophet Isaiah was talking about. He asked Philip if Isaiah was speaking of himself, or another. Philip wasted no time. **Beginning from the Scripture that the man was reading, Philip preached Jesus Christ to him, and the man became a believer.**

As they went on their way, they came upon some water and the man asked if there was any reason he could not be water baptised.

³⁷ *And Philip said, If thou believest with all thine heart, thou mayest. And he answered and said,* **I believe that**

***Jesus Christ is the Son of God**. ³⁸ And he commanded the chariot to stand still: and they went down both into the water, both Philip and the eunuch; and he baptized him.³⁹ And when they were come up out of the water, the Spirit of the Lord caught away Philip, that the eunuch saw him no more: and he went on his way rejoicing. Act 8 KJV*

I adore this portion of Scripture. Christ was revealed in the teaching and preaching of the Word of God to the Ethiopian eunuch by Philip. The man got born again on the spot, and was water baptised almost immediately after this. What is so interesting is the way this came to be.

Firstly, the angel of the Lord appeared to Philip and told him to go in a certain direction. **Philip listened and obeyed to what he was seeing prophetically.**

Secondly, the Holy Spirit then spoke to Philip and instructed him further – to go near the chariot. **Philip listened and obeyed what he was hearing prophetically from the Spirit of God.**

Thirdly, at the very moment the man was searching the Scriptures and desirous to understand them, Philip was present to answer all his questions and preach Jesus as the Christ – and because of this the man repented and was welcomed into the Kingdom of God. **Philip listened to what he was hearing prophetically, interpreted the Scriptures, and [apostolically] preached Christ.**

Fourthly, Philip water baptised the new disciple and went on his way (actually, Philip was whisked away by the Holy Spirit.) THE ETHIOPIAN BELIEVER WOULD NOW CARRY THE GOOD NEWS OF THE GOSPEL OF JESUS CHRIST AND HIS KINGDOM TO AFRICA! ***The prophetic grace, coupled with the evangelistic and teaching grace, led to Kingdom advancement.***

This is a glorious example of prophetic and apostolic preaching, teaching, and evangelism that leads to Kingdom advancement on an inter-continental, transglobal level!

We see here the realm of revelation by the Spirit, and teaching and preaching of the Word in perfect harmony! This is an example of "revival" type apostolic/prophetic preachers/teachers, who often partner (though not exclusively) with evangelist type preachers in the Body of Christ.

PART 3 – KINGDOM GOVERNANCE

CHAPTER 13 - APOSTOLIC AND PROPHETIC PRESBYTERY

"neglect not the gift that is in thee, which was given thee by prophecy, with the laying on of the hands of the Presbytery." 1 Timothy 4:14 KJV

Paul, Silas, and Timothy

In Acts Chapter 16, Paul and Silas bring a young man named Timothy into their team. This is after Paul and Barnabas have unfortunately had a falling out over John Mark, but this is later rectified and the relationships are restored (1 Peter 5:13).

Young Timothy 's mum was a Jew, but his father was a Greek. For this reason Paul decided to circumcise Timothy. Paul was fundamentally opposed to circumcision of believers after conversion, but it was just easier on this occasion to circumcise Timothy, so the work of the ministry could proceed unhindered.

Of course something must have happened in Acts Chapter 16 beyond Paul only circumcising Timothy. Paul is an apostle, and Silas is described as a prophet. Here we have the apostolic and the prophetic ascension gifts working together, bringing a new believer onto their team.

Apostolic and Prophetic Presbytery

I like in first Timothy Chapter 4 in verse 14 how Apostle Paul says, *"neglect not the gift that is in thee,* **which was** *given thee by prophecy, with the laying on of the hands of the Presbytery."* KJV

We see an example of Presbytery here. The modern day church has called it "prophetic Presbytery," but this is not wholly accurate, because it was not only prophetic. Apostle Paul is with prophet Silas, Dr Luke, and of course young Timothy at the time when Apostle Paul calls Timothy into the ministry. Apostle Paul does more than circumcise the young man. **He creates an Apostolic/Prophetic Presbytery whereby he is the lead apostle, the set man over the team, and prophet Silas is there also fully involved in the ministration to Timothy.**

Impartation

According to 1 Timothy Chapter 4 verse 14, Paul reminded Timothy about this moment of being prayed for, and prophesied over by the Presbytery - that happened in Acts Chapter 16. He received a [spiritual] gift; the gift was given by means of prophecy, <u>and</u> there was an impartation by the laying on of hands. We do not know who prophesied - whether it was apostle Paul, or whether it was prophet Silas, or if it was both of them; but we can be certain that there was both prophecy and impartation through the laying on of hands, as well as apostolic governance.

After this prayerful, apostolic, and prophetic and introduction to ministry, they continued the mission. Paul and Silas, Timothy, and probably Dr Luke is with him. They deliver the letter of Jerusalem Council - the apostles and elders which were at Jerusalem - concerning circumcision. This is a bit funny, since Paul has just circumcised Timothy, but there were good social and spiritual reasons that he did so as we have already noted above.

In commissioning/ordination services at which I am the ministering apostle, it is always my immense joy and honour to lay hands on my disciples/mentees, and pray for a release and increase of spiritual gifting, as led by the Holy Spirit. There are times when we also invite prophetic ministers to pray at this part of the service also. It is a great blessing to see spiritual sons, daughters and mentees be established and built up in their calling and gifting in and through Christ.

The Bible makes it clear that under the direction of the apostles - elders and bishops were to be appointed and ordained ... *and ordain elders in every city, as I had appointed thee: Titus 1:5b. KJV*

Impart a Spiritual Gift

Paul writes to the church in Rome, how he longed to see them so that he might impart some spiritual gift to them. So we can see that when Apostle Paul laid hands on believers, it was with an expectation that the Holy Spirit would impart a [spiritual] gift to them. This impartation was for the mutual edification of all parties. *[11] For I long to see you, that I may impart unto you some spiritual gift, to the end ye may be established;* [12] *That is, that I may be comforted together with you by the mutual faith both of you and me. Romans 1 KJV*

CHAPTER 14 - THE ANTIOCH QUESTION

[2] As they ministered to the Lord, and fasted, the Holy Ghost said, Separate me Barnabas and Saul for the work whereunto I have called them. [3] And when they had fasted and prayed, and laid their hands on them, they sent them away. Acts 13 KJV

There are many leaders today who present Antioch as either "the only" model of New Testament church, or one of the main models of New Testament church. It is, therefore, an important topic for us to consider. The answer to the Antioch question of who is ordaining who, (if indeed anyone is being ordained), will determine our understanding of the apostolic, the prophetic, and the teaching model that was functioning at the church in Antioch.

The foundation of any structure is what gives strength to the building. To understand what is constructed, we need to know its genesis i.e. the origin of same. Let's dig down a little bit together into the Scriptures surrounding the question of whether the apostles' were ordained by the prophets and teachers at Antioch.

How did the Church at Antioch begin?

After Stephen was martyred and the church was scattered as far as Phoenicia, Cyprus, and Antioch, the initial preaching during the persecution was to Jews only. Then some of those from Cyprus and Cyrene came to Antioch and spoke to the Grecians, preaching Jesus as the Christ.

Many became born again, and the number of new believers swelled (Acts 11:19-21).

When this wonderful news reached the Council of apostles and elders at Jerusalem, the Council sent forth Barnabas in response. Barnabas reached Antioch and found the new believers there, and exhorted them to remain strong in their faith (Acts 11:22-24).

Shortly after his arrival, Barnabas went to Tarsus to look for Saul and having found him there, they returned to Antioch and taught the new believers for an entire year (v25-26). *[26] And when he had found him, he brought him unto Antioch. And it came to pass, that a whole year they assembled themselves with the church, and taught much people. And the disciples were called Christians first in Antioch. KJV*

The Apostolic Foundation of the Church at Antioch

Let me point out a crucial aspect of understanding the 'Antioch model': the foundation of the church at Antioch was laid by two apostles – Barnabas and Saul (Paul). They taught Christ, and the church at Antioch had a strong Kingdom, Christ-centred doctrinal foundation. Remember I said that the foundation of a building determines what can be built upon it. *Let me say it again – the foundation of the church at Antioch was apostolic, and built on the foundation of the revelation of Christ taught by the two apostles, Paul, and Barnabas.* This is the genesis of the church at Antioch; the apostolic grace gift was the foundational DNA of the church that was raised up from there.

Acts Chapter 9 narrates the conversion of Saul. After he received his sight again because of the prayer of Ananias, and was baptised, Saul's first preaching assignment was ... [20]*And straightway he preached Christ in the synagogues, that he is the Son of God.* KJV

Antioch was not the first place that the apostles taught Christ. It continued from the pattern established prior to Apostle Paul's (Saul) conversion on the road to Damascus. However, it was at Antioch that the disciples were first called Christians i.e. Christ followers. They were not called Jesus-ians. No. The apostles taught Christ to the church for an entire year, and the believers took on His name, because they were Christ's disciples.

The Appearance of Agabus and other Prophets from Jerusalem

We are told in verses 27-28 that in those days, i.e. at some point during the first year of Apostle Paul and Barnabas teaching at Antioch and establishing the church, some prophets came from Jerusalem to Antioch and amongst their number was a man named Agabus. Agabus gave a prophetic word by the Spirit: that there would be a great dearth in the Earth, and this came to pass under the rule of Claudius Caesar.

Apostles and Prophets Together

It is clear there were no issues between the apostles and the prophets at Antioch at that time. Apostle Paul and Barnabas received Agabus and the other prophets from Jerusalem. Here we can see how the genuine prophetic gift was welcomed by the genuine apostolic ministers. The apostolic foundation made room for the prophetic ministers that came to Antioch from Jerusalem. This is an incredibly positive New Testament model for us to note. It is an example of a strategic Kingdom liaison.

They were all credible ministers, and there was no competition between the two grace gifts of apostle and prophet. The prophets did not come to disrupt the apostolic doctrinal foundation laid by the apostles, and neither did the prophets usurp the authority of the local apostolic leaders of the church at Antioch. Similarly, the apostles did not denigrate the prophetic ministers who came to be a blessing to the church. *There was mutual respect and plurality between them.* That is because there was governmental order, which was created by the apostle's doctrine. Christ was first!

'First'

There are some prophets today who suggest that God did not mean it when He said through Apostle Paul to the church at Corinth, that the apostles are in the "first place" in the church. That is possibly because they have experienced an abuse of power, or it could be simply a lack of understanding of what it means to be 'first' regarding the apostolic.

²⁸ And God hath set some in the church, first apostles, secondarily prophets, thirdly teachers, after that miracles, then gifts of healings, helps, governments, diversities of tongues. 1 Corinthians 12:28 KJV

The Greek adverb for first is *'proton'* and according to Strong's Concordance it means *firstly (in time, place, order, or importance): - before, at the beginning chiefly (at, at the) first (of all).* When first is ascribed to Christ it is *protos* meaning foremost in all things.

First to Serve

The role of apostle as 'first' is in like manner to Christ, who was first to be sent from His Father; first to serve; first to lay foundations; first to build; first to love; first to give; first to govern; first to call disciples and apostles; first as a Son over God's house, whose house are we, and importantly *He was also first to serve and to suffer for our sakes.*

The apostle is 'first' in similar dispensation of grace in their capacity to serve God and His people. To be 'first' is not about lording it over others, demanding the best seat, or the greatest accolades, but rather it is about being a son who is a servant to all as we follow Christ's example. Apostolic 'firsts' include governance; fatherhood; foundation laying; establishing; building; breakthrough; pioneering; planting, discipling, and preaching and teaching Christ to name just a few of the 'firsts' as regards to apostolic functionality.

Now let us return to the church in Antioch ... a collection was taken up, and the church agreed that Barnabas and Saul would take the offering to the elders in Jerusalem. The fact of their going to Jerusalem and returning to Antioch is confirmed in Acts 12:24, indeed they returned with John Mark.

[1]Now there were in the church at Antioch certain prophets and teachers; as **Barnabas**, and Simeon that was called Niger, and Lucius of Cyrene, and Manaen, which had been brought up with Herod the tetrarch, and **Saul.**[2] As they ministered to the Lord, and fasted, the Holy Ghost said, **Separate me Barnabas and Saul for the work whereunto I have called them.**[3] And when they had fasted and prayed, and laid their hands on them, they sent them away. Acts 13 KJV

Some interpret these verses to mean that the Apostles' Paul and Barnabas were ordained into ministry by the prophets and teachers. In my opinion this is not an accurate exegesis. Let's remember that Apostle Paul had already been serving the Lord Jesus Christ in full time ministry for circa 10-14 years before his appearing at Antioch! Indeed it was Christ Jesus Himself who commissioned Saul to be an apostle to the Gentiles (Acts 9; Acts 26:12-19; c.f. Acts 22:15).

One train of thought is that Paul and Barnabas were known only as prophets and teachers. This is not an entirely accurate interpretation. They were apostles who both taught; therefore, we can legitimately describe them as [apostolic] teachers. Paul had a great love for the prophetic, and possibly had more prophetic dreams and encounters than any other believer! Therefore the reference to them being "prophets" is more likely to be because they were apostles, who could also move in prophetic gifting. There are many examples of Apostle Paul's capacity to move in the prophetic gifting throughout the New Testament. Indeed, we have already studied some of them in this book.

Paul and Barnabas were apostles. *Firstly*, we have already established in Acts 11:26 how they taught the new disciples for an entire year at Antioch. As apostles, they taught for twelve months at Antioch prior to the instruction from the Holy Spirit to send them out on a new mission (see Acts 13:2).

Secondly, we can account for other prophets being at Antioch because we know that Agabus and other prophets arrived at Antioch after Saul and Barnabas had been there teaching the church for almost one year. (Acts 11:27-28)

Thirdly, most apostles can operate in most, or all the other spiritual gifts, which means there is no dichotomy in Apostle Barnabas and Saul (Paul) both described in the Bible as apostles, as being referred to as being amongst the teachers and prophets in the verse above.

Just one chapter later in Acts 14:14, we read how the apostles were almost made into 'gods' by the people at

Lystra. Because of the healing of an important man. ¹⁴*Which when the apostles, Barnabas and Paul, heard of, they rent their clothes, and ran in among the people crying out. KJV*

Fifth, Paul *never* refers to himself as a prophet. He only ever refers to himself as an apostle. In fact he makes this reference sixteen times in the New Testament!

- Jesus is described once as an Apostle (Hebrews 3:1);
- Peter is described twice as an apostle and servant of Jesus Christ (1 Peter 1:1, 2 Peter 1:1);
- Paul is described sixteen times as an apostle (and servant of Jesus Christ)! (Romans 1:1, 11:13; 1 Corinthians 1:1, 9:1, 2; 15:9; 2 Corinthians 1:1, 12:12; Galatians 1:1; Ephesians 1:1; Colossians 1:1; 1 Timothy 1:1; 2:7; 2 Timothy 1:1, 11; Titus 1:1)

² As they ministered to the Lord, and fasted, the Holy Ghost said, **Separate** *me Barnabas and Saul for the work whereunto I have called them.*

Critically, the Greek verb "separate" *aphorizo* means to DIVIDE, SEPARATE AND SEVER. It does NOT translate as ordain.

The Greek *Separate* [873 APHORIZO Strong's Concordance] is used only five times in the New Testament: Matthew 25:32; Luke 6:22; Acts 13:2; 2

Corinthians 6:17; Jude 19, and **always means to divide, separate, and sever**.

Since the Holy Spirit said *"separate"* Barnabas and Saul, and that it means He wanted to divide them from something, then the questions arise: 1) divide them from what? 2) Separate them from what? Since the Greek verb leaves no doubt that it is a separation (*not an ordination*), what then is the context and application? Let us remember this is the first time the church was sending out a missionary team from a local church base.

1. The **two apostles had been involved in teaching in the local church for one year** at Antioch.
2. The Holy Spirit wanted **to send the two apostles on an apostolic journey**; the new Kingdom mission work was no longer focused only on the local church. At this point Barnabas and Saul are the only apostles we are aware of at Antioch, or at least the only apostles mature enough to take on this pioneering Kingdom mission work.
3. The **new work would be trans local,** eventually becoming **transglobal - to the uttermost ends of the earth.** Jesus had instructed that it must be this way, just prior to His ascension.
4. The **Holy Spirit wanted to differentiate between local ministry and the global ministry of apostleship. THIS DIFFERENTIATION IS WHY A SEPARATION WAS NEEDED** – the apostles would no longer be resident at Antioch, but would be on the

road from this time forth, returning at times, but never settling again permanently only in one place.

5. **The Holy Spirit (not the church, or any leaders in church) chose the two apostles Barnabas and Saul,** who were carrying the grace and authority to advance the Kingdom, pioneer, plant, and teach new believers, making disciples (as the original Eleven had been instructed to do so by Christ).

6. **Because they were a team and had become a Kingdom family, the church family, and the leaders of the church family i.e. the apostles, the prophets and the teachers were all involved in praying and fasting.** They had such a great relational connectedness, a fantastic leadership governmental structure and heart and mind unity and one-ness, and all were able to hear the Voice of God, through the Holy Spirit.

7. **The apostles, the prophets, and the teachers then followed the instruction of the Holy Spirit – they BLESSED the two apostles** as they were **SENT BY THE HOLY SPIRIT** from the church at Antioch TO EMBARK ON THE FIRST TRANS LOCAL MISSION OF THE CHURCH.

8. **The apostles showed their humility, their appreciation and belief in the church family, and in the prophets and teachers who prayed for them to bless them** as they went in the name of Christ Jesus.

This is the first time the known church "sent" an apostolic team on a missionary journey; therefore it required an innovative approach, and a new setting apart.

Fundamentally, Paul was not "ordained" as an apostle at Antioch. Paul was chosen and called into ministry as a disciple and apostle when the Lord Jesus Christ encountered him on the road to Damascus. We read of his miracle conversion in Acts Chapter 9. Paul was emphatic in proclaiming that his apostleship WAS NOT OF MEN BUT GIVEN BY GOD.

As we have already noted, Paul's ministry began shortly after he had been water baptised and Spirit filled. Having refreshed himself and then spending a few days with the disciples at Damascus, he immediately began to preach in the synagogues that Jesus was the Christ, encountering massive opposition and persecution from the Jews in Jerusalem, *[20] And straightway he preached Christ in the synagogues, that he is the Son of God. Acts 9*

We can see clearly that the church at Antioch <u>did not</u> appoint, choose, or select the apostles and ordain them into ministry. *They separated* the apostles unto the work of God in agreement with the Holy Spirit, the apostles themselves, and the other leaders at the church in Antioch. Nonetheless, we joyfully acknowledge that it was an apostolic company with multi-faceted spiritual gifting that resided at Antioch, which prayed, strategised, and operated together for Kingdom advancement and redemption through Christ, to cause reformation of people, culture, and nations.

CHAPTER 15 - BUILDING TOGETHER

¹¹ Now these are the gifts Christ gave to the church: the apostles, the prophets, the evangelists, and the pastors and teachers. ¹² Their responsibility is to equip God's people to do his work and build up the church, the body of Christ. Ephesians 4 NLT

Apostle Paul's words in Ephesians Chapter 4 reveal that the ascension gifts Christ gave to the church when He ascended to His Father include apostle, prophet, shepherd, evangelist, and teacher (v11), so we understand these five grace gifts (or offices) are still active in today's church by the power of the Holy Spirit.

I like the strategic nature of the NLT version:

¹¹ Now these are the gifts Christ gave to the church: the apostles, the prophets, the evangelists, and the pastors and teachers. ¹² Their responsibility is to equip God's people to do his work and build up the church, the body of Christ. Ephesians 4 NLT

Christ Gave the Ascension Gifts to the Church

Firstly, we are clear that it is *Christ* who has given the ascension gifts to His church. These five gifts are the full representation of Christ's leadership mantle, which He has endowed to the church through the five "offices" or grace gifts that Apostle Paul refers to as:

1. Apostle
2. Prophet

3. Evangelist
4. Pastor
5. Teacher.

Secondly, we can confidently assert that these spiritual gifts are ASCENSION GIFTS – meaning it is the Lord Jesus Christ Himself who gave them as gifts of leadership to the church at His ascension to the right hand of the Father. Describing or emphasising the "ascension" aspect of the five-fold offices above, helps us immensely to differentiate them from any other spiritual leadership gift (prophet or otherwise) that existed before the death, resurrection, and ascension of Christ.

The Corporate Responsibility of the Ascension Gifts to Equip God's People

¹² *Their responsibility is to equip God's people to do his work and build up the church, the body of Christ.* Ephesians 4 NLT

Thirdly, we cannot fail to notice that these five ascension gifts [or offices] have ONE CORPORATE RESPONSIBILITY TOGETHER to equip God's people to do God's work and build up the church.

It is not that the apostle has one responsibility and the other four offices do not; neither is it that the prophet has one responsibility, and the evangelist and pastor are excluded from the equipping ministry. No. All five ascension gifts [or offices] are corporately responsible before God for aligning, equipping, empowering, and discipling the church – that is the entire body of Christ – for the work of God, and the building up to maturity of the body of Christ.

<u>We</u> – the apostles, prophets, evangelists, pastors, and teachers - <u>are responsible</u> <u>together</u> to ensure that God's people are rightly aligned, positioned, trained, and equipped i.e. discipled. And that Christ be revealed in, to, and through the church; and that each fivefold ministry office [ascension gift] does their part in the process. It is a glorious, and necessary call to oneness in the fivefold.

We simply cannot stress enough the critical nature of unity and oneness, operating from the foundation of the revelation of Christ, His love, the Spirit and the Word of God in Kingdom building, advancement, and discipleship. We need a mind shift and a new mind-set that radically moves away from the notion of superstardom and big egos, whether they be apostles, prophets, teachers, evangelists, or pastors! All should humbly be involved in edification, exhortation, comforting, strengthening and discipleship of the church global.

Strategic Nature of Engagement

We always encourage the pastors and leaders in our New Destiny Global Ministries leadership network to build big people! That does not mean massage people's egos; it means to invest strategically in those whom God has entrusted to your sphere of influence. Be secure and mature as a leader, and disciple and raise others up to their full potential in Christ.

All fivefold ministers are needed to develop and disciple mature, well balanced, equipped, fruitful ministers within the body of Christ for church ministration, and for marketplace ministration.

All fivefold ministers are needed in Kingdom building and Kingdom advancement, albeit each must take their God-given place and specific role within the Kingdom for maximum impact, influence, and transformation of individuals, cultures, cities, and nations. Albeit apostolic ministers have a particular grace for Kingdom building.

Not All Prophets are the Same!

Some prophets are more word oriented (*"nabi"*); others are more visionary "seers," whilst still others operate in strong gift of discernment – not necessarily discerning of spirits, but of directional discernment.

Not every prophet operates in the same sphere; they have a different "reach," whether that is local, regional, national, or global. Some are called to church-based ministry, whilst others are called to engage in the marketplace sector.

Not all prophets have the same focus/remit. Some are much more strategically minded, and work well with apostles in vision/mission consolidation, and implementation. These are sometimes referred to as *"reformation prophets,"* by modern day commentators. The Antioch church model we looked at is an example of strategic, governmental engagement by the five-fold ascension gifts, including the apostle, the prophet, and the teacher.

Other prophets have a strong word of knowledge gifting and work well in evangelistic outreach settings, also moving in the gift of healing. These types of prophets are sometimes referred to as *"revival prophets"* by commentators today. Our brief study of Philip and the Ethiopian eunuch gives us a New Testament example of prophecy, evangelism, and teaching operating in a mutually beneficial Kingdom mode.

CONCLUSION

We have almost reached the end of our panoramic journey looking through the lens of the New Testament [from an apostolic perspective,] of how the prophetic ministry has evolved, and been transformed through Christ in the new covenant of Grace.

We set out to study the matrix [environment and culture], in which the prophetic developed in the early New Testament church. This included: -

- Prophetic predictive foretelling
- General prophecy to the church
- Dream/Vision in the night
- Visions – these include both "seeing" and "hearing" spiritually.
- Trance
- Encounters with Christ
- Angelic visitation/angelic intervention
- Open Heaven
- Discernment/knowing.

We have successfully looked at New Testament examples of all the above, chiefly through the Gospels and the Acts of the Apostles. I have also shared some leadership experiences and insights, which we have gained through our work in the nations, training and equipping leaders and believers, and discipling the Body of Christ over the last three decades.

Through Scripture we can now understand that the Old Testament office of prophet is closed; and the New Testament ascension gift of prophet in Christ is vastly different to the Old Testament remit of the prophets, since they were under the dispensation of the Law. We have established that we can now all "prophesy" because we are sons in Christ under the new covenant of Grace.

Along the way we have also considered some of the damage that [false] prophets and [false] teachers have caused in the body of Christ, but we are focused on the love of God and in moving deeper in our relationship with Christ, and in the gifts the Holy Spirit has for us in the Kingdom of God. God still has a faithful remnant in our day!

Let's remind ourselves that the Classic Edition of the (AMPC) version describes the role of the New Testament prophet as, *"inspired interpreters of the will and purposes of God,"* 1 Corinthians 12:29.

We concluded that the New Testament prophet is to 1. Reveal Christ, and 2. teach believers how to understand, and interpret the divine will and purpose of God in their lives. This has both an individual, and a corporate application for believers and the church. It can manifest in church settings, and also in the marketplace environment.

It's All About Christ

The prophets of the Old Testament were prophesying about Christ, and when He came He fulfilled their prophecies in His coming: the testimony of Jesus the Son of man, [who is also Christ, the Son of God] is the spirit of prophecy. The King James Version states, *[10] And I fell at his feet to worship him. And he said unto me, See thou do it not: I am thy fellowservant, and of thy brethren that have the testimony of Jesus: worship God: <u>for the testimony of Jesus is the spirit of prophecy.</u> Revelation 19*

The essence (or core reason) for prophecy is to give a clear and undeniable witness that Jesus is the Christ – the testimony of Jesus is the spirit of prophecy.

Jesus Christ fulfilled the Law and the Prophets, *[17] Think not that I am come to destroy the law, or the prophets: I am not come to destroy, but to fulfil. Matthew 5 KJV*

The Law is fulfilled by Christ's sacrificial death and resurrection on behalf of mankind. He is the Mediator of the new covenant of Grace, and has fulfilled every aspect of the Law by His sacrifice at the Cross.

- The prophets are fulfilled because Jesus Christ is the testimony of their prophecy (Revelation 19:10).
- The Person that the Old Testament prophets pointed to was CHRIST.
- The divine Purpose of the Old Testament prophets pointing to CHRIST was to REVEAL CHRIST;
- And to be A WITNESS FOR CHRIST, and when Christ came He fulfilled their prophecies at His coming.

We cannot end without reminding ourselves of the importance of Love, without which no spiritual gift has any value, or can produce any kind of fruit that will last for eternity, *¹³ And now abideth faith, hope, charity, these three; but the greatest of these is charity. 1 Corinthians 13*

We bless the Lord that as He ascended into Heaven, He gave the full representation of Himself to the church, and through the church, the five ascension gifts of apostle, prophet, teacher, evangelist, and pastor will equip the believers to reshape the landscape of the nations with Heaven's Kingdom agenda. It is the corporate responsibility of all five ascension gifts to equip, empower and mature the saints for works of service, and to attain the full measure of the stature of Christ as a corporate man.

Unity and oneness of focus, heart, and mind are critical to our successfully fulfilling the Great Commission. Everyone has a unique call in Christ, and is graced with spiritual gifting to be a blessing wherever they are planted. *²⁰ When I am raised to life again, you will know that I am in my Father, and you are in me, and I am in you. John 14 NLT*

Let Christ be our All in All

As we end our present study on the matrix of the New Testament gift of prophecy (in Christ), let us remind ourselves of this glorious and crucial truth that whilst all may prophesy – our relationship with Christ is more important than any other relationship, or any other gift.

He is the Gift that God gave to the world, to save us from our sin, and make us sons of God and heirs through Christ.

Our Heavenly Father has commissioned and anointed us to reveal Christ Jesus our Lord and Saviour in every nation of the earth, and in every sphere of society. The Old Testament prophets all pointed to Christ, may we the church continue to emulate this and reveal our Beloved Christ Jesus our Lord, the Darling of Heaven, the Bright Morning Star in the nations of the Earth.

The revelation of Christ is more than evangelism; Christ is the Mystery now revealed in, to, and through the church (1 Corinthians 2:6-8; Ephesians 3:9-10; Colossians 1:26-27). Importantly, it is also about discipleship that leads to personal and societal transformation. Apostle John speaks in his second epistle of 1) the Person of Christ and 2) the Doctrine of Christ. To deny either is to be anti-Christ (2 John 1:7-10).

This book has been about endorsing and teaching what I believe is the New Testament model for prophecy in and through Christ, and by His Holy Spirit. It is my earnest hope that all who read this book will see the matrix of the prophetic through this [apostolic] lens, and that it will help to re-calibrate our hearts and minds to reveal Christ and His Kingdom – whether through apostolic preaching and teaching, prophetic grace, or any other spiritual gift.

May the Holy Spirit enable us to operate in Truth and grace; may the love of the Father dwell deeply in our hearts; and may our Beloved Christ be revealed in and through all as we build together for His glory.

The grace of our Lord Jesus Christ be with you all. Amen

Apostle Catherine Brown

APPENDICES
APPENDIX 1 - MESSIANIC PROPHECIES FULFILLED IN CHRIST (NOT AN EXHAUSTIVE LIST)

SCRIPTURE STATING PROPHECY	SUBJECT OF PROPHECY	SCRIPTURE STATING FULFILLMENT
Genesis 3:15	Born of the seed of a woman	Galatians 4:4
Genesis 12:2-3	Born of the seed of Abraham	Matthew 1:1
Genesis 17:19	Born of the seed of Isaac	Matthew 1:2
Numbers 24:17	Born of the seed of Jacob	Matthew 1:2
Genesis 49:10	Descended from tribe of Judah	Luke 3:33
Isaiah 9:7	Heir to the throne of David	Luke 1:32-33
Daniel 9:25	Time for Jesus' birth	Luke 2:1-2
Isaiah 7:14	Born of a virgin	Luke 1:26-27; 30-31
Micah 5:2	Born in Bethlehem	Luke 2:4-7
Jeremiah 31:15	Slaughter of the innocents	Matthew 2:16-18
Hosea 11:1	Flight to Egypt	Matthew 2:14-15
Isaiah 40:3-5; Malachi 3:1	Preceded by a forerunner	Luke 7:24, 27
Psalm 2:7	Declared the Son of God	Matthew 3:16-17
Isaiah 9:1-2	Galilean ministry	Matthew 4:13-17
Deuteronomy 18:15, 18	The prophet to come	Acts 3:20, 22
Isaiah 61:1-2	Came to heal the broken-hearted	Luke 4:18-19
Isaiah 53:3	Rejected by His own (the Jews)	John 1:11
Psalm 110:4	A priest after the order of Melchizedek	Hebrews 5:5-6
Zechariah 9:9	Triumphal entry	Mark 11:7, 9, 11
Psalm 41:9	Betrayed by a friend	Luke 22:47, 48

Zechariah 11:12-13	Sold for thirty pieces of silver	Matthew 26:15; 27:5-7
Psalm 35:11	Accused by false witnesses	Mark 14:57-58
Isaiah 53:7	Silent to accusations	Mark 15:4, 5
Isaiah 50:6	Spat upon and smitten	Matthew 26:67
Psalm 35:19	Hated without reason	John 15:24, 25
Isaiah 53:5	Vicarious sacrifice	Romans 5:6, 8
Isaiah 53:12	Crucified with transgressors	Mark 15:27, 28
Zechariah 12:10	Hands pierced	John 20:27
Psalm 22:7-8	Scorned and mocked	Luke 23:35
Psalm 69:21	Given vinegar and gall	Matthew 27:34
Psalm 109:4	Prayer for his enemies	Luke 23:34
Psalm 22:18	Soldiers gambled for his coat	Matthew 27:35
Psalm 34:20	No bones broken	John 19:32-33, 36
Zechariah 12:10	Side pierced	John 19:34
Isaiah 53:9	Buried with the rich	Matthew 27:57-60
Psalm 16:10; 49:15	Would rise from the dead	Mark 16:6-7
Psalm 68:18	Would ascend to God's right hand	Mark 16:19

APPENDIX 2 - TABLE OF PROPHETIC ACTIVITY FROM THE BOOK OF ACTS

OPEN VISION / VISION – "SEE" "HEAR"	PREDICTIVE / FORETELLING	PROPHECY GENERAL	TRANCE	DREAM / VISION IN NIGHT	ENCOUNTER – WITH CHRIST OR ANGEL	DISCERNMENT / KNOWING
Deacon Stephen martyred; he saw heaven opened and prayed for mercy for his persecutors, including Saul (Acts 7:55-60)	Prophet Agabus comes from Jerusalem to Antioch with other prophets, and he prophesied (Acts 11:27-28)	Prophets Judas and Silas exhort and encourage the congregation at Antioch (Acts 15:32-35)	Ap Peter fell into a trance, vision x 3 prior to Caesarea, where the Gentiles receive Holy Spirit (Acts 10:9-20 c.f. Acts 11:5-18)	Ap Paul's "Macedonian Call" sent the team into Europe to preach the Gospel for the first time (Acts 16:6-10)	Angel releases the apostles from prison in Jerusalem, they return to preach Christ (Acts 5:19-20)	Ap Peter discerns Ananias and Sapphira have lied to Holy Spirit; they both drop down dead within three hours of each other (Acts 5:1-11)
Ap Paul concerning Ananias/ Ananias' vision re Paul; Paul receives his sight and is baptised	Agabus prophesied to Paus but Paul gives him proper context for interpretation (Acts 21:10-14)	Ephesus - Twelve new believers receive baptism by Ap Paul and they receive the Holy Spirit and	Ap Paul prayed in temple, fell into a trance, then the Lord warned him to	Ap Paul in Corinth, God speaks to him in a dream to reassure him and he stays for a further eighteen	Christ encounters Saul on the road to Damascus. He is born again and begins to preach	Ap Peter discerns the heart of Simon the (former sorcerer); he repents and is convicted asking for prayer

(Acts 9:10-19)		prophesy. (Acts 19:1-7)	get out of Jerusalem. (Acts 22:17-21)	months (Acts 18:9-11)	Jesus as the Christ (Acts 9:1-22)	(Acts 8:18-25)
Philip hears the voice of Holy Spirit instructing him to go and speak to the Ethiopian (Acts 8:29)		Philip the evangelist had four daughters who prophesy (Acts 21:8-9)			Angel appears to Cornelius, instructs him to send men to Joppa for Ap Peter (Acts 10:1-8; 30-33)	Ap Paul warns the Ephesian elders of savage wolves "For I know …" (Acts 20:29:30)
					The angel of the Lord releases Ap Peter from prison after Herod had murdered Ap James (Acts 12:1-19)	Ap Paul perceives the ship will wreck but they will survive (Acts 27:10)
					The Lord appears to Ap Paul and tells him to testify "in Rome"	Ap Paul perceived the crippled man at Lystra had faith

						as he had done Jerusalem (Acts 23:11)	to be healed (Acts 14:8-10)
						Angel appears to Ap Paul and told him they will be safely cast onto an island (Acts 27:23-26)	Ap Paul perceived the Council that had united together to oppose him was comprised of both Pharisees and Sadducees (Acts 23:6)

APPENDIX 3 – PROPHECIES IN THE GOSPELS CONCERNING CHRIST'S BIRTH/EARLY DAYS

PROPHECY	DREAM	ENCOUNTER
Elizabeth prophesies over Mary whilst she they are both pregnant (Luke 1:39-45)	Wise men receive a dream warning them not to return to Herod (Matthew 2:12)	Joseph angelic visitation instructed to marry Mary and about the birth of Christ the Son of God (Matthew 1:20; 1:18-25)
Mary's song - The Magnificat (Luke 1:46-56)	Angel appeared to Joseph and warned him to take his family into Egypt (Matthew 2:13-15)	Angel appears to Zechariah at the temple to announce the birth of John the Baptist to he and his wife Elizabeth (Luke 1:11-25)
Zechariah's prophecy concerning Christ and the forerunner John the Baptist (Luke 1:67-79)	Joseph instructed by the angel that Herod was dead and he should return to Israel with his family (Matthew 2:19-21)	Mary and the angel Gabriel – birth of Jesus foretold (Luke 1:26-38)
Simeon prophesies over Christ on the day of his circumcision (Luke 2:22-35)	Joseph warned in a dream not to go to Judaea and he went to Nazareth instead (Matthew 1:22-23)	The shepherds and the angels, at Christ's birth (Luke 2:8-21)
Anna - the widow - prophesies over the baby Christ at the temple in like manner to Simeon (Luke 2:37-38)		When John encounters Christ he states He is the Lamb of God and the Son of God (John 1:26-34; 36)

APPENDIX 4 – GOSPEL OF MATTHEW/JESUS CHRIST

ANNOUNCEMENT	PROPHECY / FORETELLING	DISCERNMENT / KNOWING
GOSPEL OF MATTHEW		
Christ announced He had come to fulfil the law and the prophets (Matthew 5:17-18)	Jesus Christ warned His disciples of persecution (Matthew 10:16-33)	Jesus saw the faith of the friends of the paralytic (Matthew 9:2)
Christ taught He will reject some who prophesied, did deliverance, or did miracles (Matthew 7:21-23)	Jesus foretells He would be three days and three nights in the heart of the earth (Matthew 12:40)	Jesus knew the Pharisees wanted to kill him after he healed the man with a withered hand; He withdrew from them (Matthew 12:9-21)
Jesus testified of John that the law and the prophets were until John, … until now the Kingdom is preached (Matthew 11:7-19)	Christ foretells His suffering, death, and resurrection (Matthew 16:21)	Christ discerns Satan influencing Simon Peter and rebuked him (Matthew 16:22-23)
Christ Jesus affirms Simon Peter has rightly heard from the Father that He is the Son of God. (Matthew 16:16-20)	Christ foretells His betrayal, death, and resurrection for a second time (Matthew 17:22-23)	Christ tells the disciples where to find the colt on which He shall enter Jerusalem on Palm Sunday (Matthew 21:2-7)
Christ casts out the money lenders at the temple quoting Isaiah 56:7 (Matthew 21:12-17)	Christ foretells His death a third time (Matthew 20:17-19)	Christ tells the disciples where to find the room to eat at the Lord's Supper (Matthew 26:17:19)
Christ quotes David's Psalm 16 concerning Himself (Son of God - Christ) Matthew 22:41-46	Jesus foretells the destruction of the Temple (Matthew 24:1-2)	Jesus identified His betrayer Judas Iscariot amongst the Twelve (Matthew 26:20-25)
	Jesus foretells the	Christ discerns the

	signs of the ends of the Age: deception, false christs,' wars, offence, betrayal, cold love, preaching of Kingdom (Matthew 24:3-14)	hour of His betrayal has come upon Him just prior to His arrest (Matthew 26:46)
	Jesus foretells of the time of Tribulation at the ends of the age, with false christs, false prophets and false miracle workers (Matthew 24:15-28)	Jesus tells Peter to get a fish in which there will be a coin to pay the Temple tax (Matthew 17:24-27)
	Christ Jesus foretells His second coming (Matthew 24:29-31)	
	Jesus foretells the Rapture and coming judgement/ eternal damnation (Matthew 24:36-51)	
	Jesus foretells the judgement of nations, reward for the righteous and eternal damnation for those not in Christ (Matthew 25:31-46)	
	Jesus foretells His disciples He will go to Galilee after His resurrection (Matthew 26:32)	
	Jesus foretells Peter's denial (Matthew 26:30-35)	
	Jesus tells Caiaphas that He will see the	

| | Son of man sitting on the right hand of God, coming in power (Matthew 26:64) | |

ABOUT THE AUTHOR

Apostle Catherine Brown is the Founding Director of New Destiny Global Ministries (NDGM). She is a strategic Kingdom builder and has almost 30 years of experience in global ministry, mission, and discipleship. In the last 2.5 years alone, the ministry has trained and equipped more than 6,000 leaders in the NDGM network.

Catherine holds an Honorary Degree in Practical Ministry D.Min. She is based in the West coast of Scotland, but spends most of her time travelling and serving in the nations. The ministry has an office in Kampala, Uganda, East Africa.

Catherine and her fellow directors, team, and partners disciple leaders and deliver strategic apostolic teaching through their developing leadership networks in East Africa and throughout the nations. They are passionate about equipping and empowering disciples, with a special emphasis on leaders.

They have ministered in Africa, USA, Mexico, South America, Australia, Asia, Europe, and UK.

Catherine is a respected Bible teacher, a preacher and a prolific author of many published books including: -
"Women in Christ;"
"The Master Discipler - Jesus Christ of Nazareth;"
The Imperfect Leader;"
"The Invested Leader;"
"Simply Apostolic Volumes 1, 2, and 3;"
"God's Wonder Women;" to name just a few.
Her books are available via Amazon.

Catherine is also an experienced concept and content Book Editor and Author Coach with many happy clients. She has authored a book to assist writers in their writing process entitled, "Author Coach - Write Your Best Non Fiction Book."

Catherine has four grown up children and lives in the West coast of Scotland.

www.newdestinyglobalministries.co.uk

catherine@newdestinyglobalministries.co.uk

Facebook: Catherine-Brown-509043002615968/

YouTube: Apostle Catherine Brown

Twitter: NewDestinyGM

OTHER BOOKS BY THE AUTHOR

Catherine's books are available on Amazon. Her latest books this year include "Women in Christ," and "Delivered!." Don't miss these life-changing reads!

Women in Christ

Catherine Brown

DELIVERED!
CATHERINE BROWN

THE MASTER DISCIPLER
CATHERINE BROWN

The Invested Leader

By Catherine Brown

GOD'S WONDER WOMEN Part 1
CATHERINE BROWN

The Imperfect Leader
(and those we serve)
By Catherine Brown

UNDERSTANDING THE KINGDOM OF GOD
CATHERINE BROWN

Simply Apostolic
Volume 1
Catherine Brown

Kingdom
Building
Realising Vision and
Developing Leaders
Catherine Brown